Out of Transylvania

A Spiritual Journey

Maria Kräutner

Copyright © 2021 by Maria Kräutner
All rights reserved.

Dedicated To

Kurt and Ernst,

and all the children of the world, striving,

in this section of time, to find meaning in their lives.

In the fullness of time,

they will *know* they are Infinite Love,

and we are All One.

PREFACE

This is my personal story and spiritual journey as a Transylvanian Saxon refugee from Romania to Austria, Canada, and then to the United States. It is not a historical rendering of my life experience but rather a remembrance of some of the positive and negative experiences of my life from when I was a small child to the present. *It reflects my state of consciousness at that time.* The individuals in my story are real, and the spoken word is from what I can remember. The places and dates are from my relatives, friends, and a little research.

Many of my experiences are common to all refugees coming to America from their war-torn countries. Research tells us that it takes three generations for children born to refugees to be fully assimilated into the American culture. To protect and insulate my two children, I attempted to accomplish this in one generation.

While both my sons were born in this country to refugee parents, I worked diligently at raising them to be happy, carefree Americans. I tried hard not to impose my baggage of the fear-driven adolescent years that I lived through, during, and after World War II. I did not disclose to them their Saxon history and heritage for fear it would somehow damage them. They were not going to be second-class citizens as I had been growing up—not if I could help it.

When I left the Lutheran Church, I took them out of Sunday school and church because I disliked the teachings of sin, hell, and damnation. Although I had nothing else to offer them, at the time I concluded that *nothing* was better than what the Church was teaching.

If I would have shared my story with my children during their formative and adolescent years, I believe it would have been a burden to them. However, my history is also their history, and at this stage of their lives, they have a right to know it.

My journey is a story of fear, betrayal, courage, and self-reliance—a journey to love.

BACKGROUND

My ancestors were Saxons, living in Transylvania, known in German as Siebenbürgen, meaning "seven castles or fortresses." The seven major cities in Transylvania were, in German, Hungarian, and Romanian:

Bistritz – Bistrita – Beszterce
Hermannstadt – Sibiu – Nagyszeben
Klausenburg – Clug-Napoca – Kolosvar
Kronstadt – Brasov – Brasso
Mediasch – Medias – Medgyes
Mulback – Sebes – Szaszsebes
Schassburg – Sighisoara – Segesvar

When viewed by satellite, Transylvania is surrounded by the mighty Carpathian Mountains. Dense forests cover the Carpathians. Regardless from which direction a visitor enters Transylvania, the land is surrounded by forests. It lies beyond the forests (Latin: trans-silva; hence, Transylvania).

For more than eight hundred years, Siebenbürgen was home to ethnic Germans who began settling the area in the twelfth century, by invitation of King Geiza II and King Andreas II. Saxons flourished and grew in power under seven different political systems.

"The Diploma Andreanum or Golden Charter was issued by King Andrew II of Hungary in 1224, granting provisional autonomy to these colonial Germans residing in Siebenbürgen, a region of the Kingdom of Hungary, (present-day area of Sibiu, Romania)." www.britannica.com

From "Saxons Through Seventeen Centuries" – John Foisel

Left – Part of the official Saxon Crest by King Ludwig the Great (1342-1381)

Center – Ancient Seal of the Transylvanian Saxons – King Andreas of Hungary made special mention of it in the 1224 Golden Charter.

Right – "Some scholars say this sign was the crest of the ancient Low German tribes. In the long and perilous history of Saxons the fortress became symbolic of the deepest values in Saxon experience. It is therefore proper that this symbol of common defense, and symbol of the German name of the country "Siebenbürgen," should constitute the Crest of the Nation."

The Saxon dialect spoken by Transylvanian Saxons is closest to the Moselle Franconian group of West Central German dialects and shares a consistent amount of lexical similarities with Luxembourgish. www.Wikipedia.com

Saxons were Catholic until the Reformation in the 16th century. Martin Luther, a monk (1483-1546), attacked the

Pope and the domination of the Roman Catholic Church. This resulted in all Saxons becoming Evangelical-Lutheran. Hungarians were Catholic, and Romanians remained Greek Orthodox.

After 1918, Saxon privileges along with their autonomy and identity were gradually diminishing until, after WWII, they were non-existent.

During WWII, in view of the advancing Russian Army, Romania switched sides, signed a truce on August 23, 1944, and declared war on Germany. Romania agreed to take up arms against its former Axis partner, in exchange for the postwar return of Transylvania to Romanian authorities.

Saxons were specifically excluded from the promised rights for minorities in 1945. Never again were Saxons allowed any kind of rights, not even over their own property in their homeland. Saxons who remained would be trapped and at the mercy of communist rule.

Our homes, property and land were confiscated by the Romanian Government, and given to their people. Romanians had often felt like second-class citizens in their own country because Saxons were the privileged "worker bees," who built the important cities in Transylvania, along with the fortified churches and castles, now used as tourist attractions.

Even the Bran Castle, on which Bram Stoker based his fictional castle when he wrote Dracula, was completed by Transylvanian Saxons in 1388 under King Louis I of Hungary.
www.britannica.com

Starting in 1978 to 1989, Germany paid a ransom of seven thousand marks for each Saxon that Mr. Ceausescu allowed to emigrate annually from Romania. www.nytimes.com1990/12/28

In 1989 after the Berlin Wall came down, my Uncle Alzner's family was finally able to leave Transylvania, Romania. He and his family had been trapped there since 1944 under communist rule. They immigrated to Germany.

In 2014, Klaus Iohannis, born in the historic centre of Sibiu, was elected the fourth president of Romania, since December 1989. He was reelected in 2019. His native language is Transylvanian Saxon. www.wikipedia.org

TABLE OF CONTENTS

1. Out of Transylvania 1
2. The War Years 8
3. The Austrian Cottage 16
4. World War II Ends 20
5. Life in the Austrian Cottage 24
6. Emigrating From Austria 29
7. The Refugee in Canada 35
8. Scripting 45
9. Work – Wedding – Married Life 55
10. Coming to America 60
11. Raising Two Boys As Americans 65
12. Firing God 70
13. A Gift of Grace 73
14. A Radical Change in Attitude 84
15. Falling In Love 92
16. Life after Divorce 99
17. The "Joy" of Traveling 104
18. Meeting Neville 118
19. The Law According to Neville 121
20. Testing the Law 127

1. OUT OF TRANSYLVANIA

My ancestors were Saxons, (ethnic Germans) living in a region called Transylvania in Romania. I was born in the village of Botsch (Batos) in Romania. Transylvania in German is Siebenbürgen, meaning "seven castles or fortresses." At the time, the cities in this region had German names. After World War II, these names all but disappeared. The Background page at the beginning of the book has a more detailed but condensed history of Siebenbürgen (Transylvania) over the many centuries to the present day.

In 1911, my grandfather left the town of Botsch, Romania, to come to the United States, shortly after the birth of his first daughter, Susanna. His destination was Youngstown, Ohio. His goal was to work in the sugar beet fields. Grandmother joined him about a year later. At that time, Youngstown was home to a large population of ethnic Germans known as Saxons.

They felt comfortable among people with the same language and history. Susanna, their firstborn, remained in the care of her grandmother back home in Transylvania. Like many others, my grandparents' plan was to work, save their money, and return home to build their dream house.

This Youngstown experience took the better part of ten years. Three more children were born to them during this time – John, George, and my mother, Mary.

Upon returning home to Botsch, they bought enough property to accommodate three houses, with acres of vineyards as far as the eye could see. On the homestead property, they built a huge barn filled with horses, cows, pigs, and chickens. They enjoyed fruit trees and a huge vegetable garden. The hemp grown there was spun into yarn on the family spinning wheel and woven into cloth. The cloth was then sewn to make clothes, bed sheets, and pillowcases. There was a loom in the barn for making colorful blankets and floor mats. Kerosene lamps lit the nights since there was no electricity.

John, the oldest of the three American-born, had difficulty adjusting to this new Saxon culture. He was constantly punished for hiding behind the barn with his brother and sister so they could talk to each other in English. English was the only language they knew.

Grandmother wanted them to speak Saxon with their oldest sibling, Susanna, and then German when they went to church or school. Romanian wasn't mandatory until fifth grade.

John disliked his life so much he decided to return to Ohio by himself at the tender age of 17. Susanna remained estranged from her three American siblings for her entire life. She married early and well and left the house to build her own family.

After completion of the homestead in 1922-1923 and before leaving for South America, my grandfather decided he wanted my mother, Mary, to be married and settled like his elder daughter, Susanna. He arranged a marriage for her with a very wealthy man. At first, my mother resisted, but my grandfather refused to take no for an answer, and he insisted until my mother finally gave in.

My mother hated being married to this man, so she ran away after only a few weeks into the marriage. In 1938, she filed for divorce. This was unheard of in our little town.

When the judge asked her what she wanted out of this marriage, she replied, "Nothing, your honor." He then asked

1. OUT OF TRANSYLVANIA

her why she wanted the divorce. "Because I just don't like the man," she replied. So, she got her divorce to her father's dismay and disapproval.

Soon after her divorce, she met my father, Johann, a shepherd, while he was taking care of a flock of sheep. He was by far the most handsome man in the town, and she fell madly in love with him. Unfortunately, he was also the poorest man in town. As a herder of sheep, he earned little money. With no education and no skills, he could barely support himself, much less a wife.

A few months later, my mother discovered she was pregnant. Scared and desperate, she did not know what to do. If she told her mother, her father would find out. If she did not tell her mother, they would eventually find out anyway.

Somehow, Grandfather found out she was pregnant. That day, sitting patiently with an axe positioned visibly on the table, he waited for his daughter to come home. When she came through the door, he picked up the axe and started toward her. Terrified, Mary turned and ran out of the house into the cold winter night.

Grandfather was angry with her for shaming him. This was more than he could bear. Everyone in town knew she had divorced the husband he had chosen for her and now *this*. Fortunately, Mary ran faster than her father and outdistanced him, disappearing into the dark.

With no money and no place to live, my mother was beside herself. The shepherd and my mother could not afford a baby. My father, Johann, could not afford to support a wife much less a baby. The only solution was for Mary to have an abortion.

But abortions were illegal. Uncle Alzner was a physician, but my mother did not dare ask him for help nor did she think that any other doctor would perform an abortion, regardless of the circumstances. Did she have the nerve to go through with an abortion? What else could she do? Sadly, Mary concluded, there were no other options but to do it herself.

When my father heard of her plans, he forbade her to do anything to their baby. When she insisted, he reasoned with her until he convinced her not to perform an abortion on herself.

Grandfather disowned her. Mary never again set foot in her father's house while he was alive. Susanna, her sister and her husband, George, took pity on my parents and allowed them to move in with them.

It was December of 1938. A few months later, against my grandfather's wishes, my parents, Mary and Johann, were married. My parents stayed with my mother's sister and her husband through the spring and summer. I was born at the end of summer that year. Two years later, my sister, Susanna, was born. Our family struggled, living in a dirt floor hut while my father tried to carve out a meager existence for us.

Mary Kräutner (Gramelt) Susanna on lap -1942- Johann Kräutner, Maria on lap
Mary 1918-1994   Johann 1916-1980

1. OUT OF TRANSYLVANIA

Devotion to God and the Evangelical Lutheran Church were a huge part of our daily life. Everyone in town knew each other by name, and we all attended church regularly. Even our minister was Saxon. "God forbid, God forgive me, God protect me, God help me," was on the lips of my mother and grandmother every day all day long. God came into our conversation often.

Early on, I learned to fear this angry, vengeful God who only seemed to punish people and never rewarded them for being good. As I grew older, my fear only intensified, as did my anger and disappointment with God.

One of my earliest memories involves my grandfather's funeral, which I was not allowed to attend. I watched from a neighbor's house across the street. Grandfather came home from South America, where he had gone to work to spend his dying days at the homestead. He was buried on a hill under a huge oak tree on the property for which he had worked so hard in America.

Johann Gramelt 1887–1943 (Grandfather)

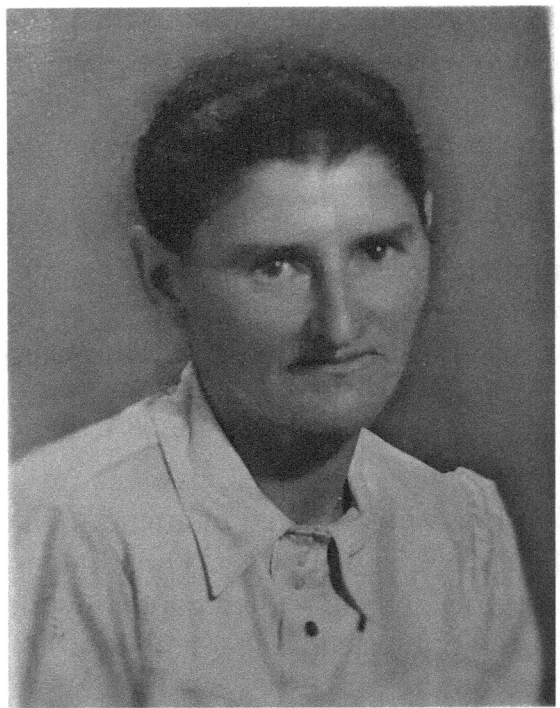

Susanna Gramelt (Alzner) 1893-1984 (Grandmother) – Mother's name (Wagner)

Gramelt Homestead - 1922-23 - #284 Batos, Romania

1. OUT OF TRANSYLVANIA

**My Mother Mary Gramelt as a Teenager
1918-1994**

Saxon Spinning Wheel

Susanna and Maria Kräutner - 1943

2. THE WAR YEARS

During the years 1940-1943, World War II was raging. Uncle John in Ohio enlisted in the American Army. Uncle George and my father were conscripted into the German Army in Transylvania, Romania. With both men gone, my mother moved our family back to the homestead to put a roof over our heads and to help Grandmother run the farm. Meanwhile, the war was not going well for the German side.

**John Gramelt 1913-1981-
The American Son**

**George Gramelt 1916-1992-
The German Son**

In view of the advancing Russian Army, Romania switched sides on August 24, 1944, and declared war on

2. THE WAR YEARS

Germany. Romania agreed to take up arms against its former Axis partner in exchange for the postwar return of Transylvania to Romanian authorities. Saxons, along with all other ethnic Germans, instantly became the enemy of the people with whom they had peacefully coexisted for hundreds of years. Some of our Romanian "friends" suddenly saw us as the enemy and did not speak to us anymore. A week later, on August 30, 1944, the Red Army occupied the Romanian capital of Bucharest south of Transylvania, as well as the valuable oil fields of Ploesti.

Artur Phleps, a highly decorated German general in the Waffen-SS, knew firsthand just how badly the war was going. Phleps served in militaries of three different countries—Austria-Hungary, Romania, and Nazi-Germany. Phleps, born near Hermannstadt in Transylvania, feared for the fate of his countrymen and ordered the immediate evacuation of Saxons in Nösnerland (Northern Transylvania).

On September 11,1944, the residents of Botsch were given two hours to pack and evacuate the town. This did not come as a complete surprise. After the D-Day invasion on the Western Front and the continuing deterioration of the Eastern Front, rumors of a possible evacuation grew louder.

Most Botschers had already repaired and overhauled their wagons. Now our worst fears were being realized. We were instructed not to take too many items because we were to be transported out of the country by train. To allay our fears, the authorities told us the move was only temporary and that we would return within a few months. Nothing could have been further from the truth.

Quickly, my mother and grandmother packed our wagon with blankets, sheets, pillows, pillowcases, clothes, pots and pans, onions, potatoes, flour, as much as the wagon could hold. With the young men gone, the exodus consisted of very old men, women, and children. Most of the work fell on the women and children.

Our horses were called to the German cavalry, so Mother hitched oxen to the front of the covered wagon and tied a cow to the back for our milk. From inside the wagon, I watched as Mother hurriedly closed the gate to the now-abandoned homestead. Grandmother was sitting up front, rocking my sister in her arms. "Herr behat, Herr behat" (God forbid, God forbid) she kept repeating over and over in Saxon as she held Susanna in her arms. Mother grabbed the harness on the ox and began walking down the street. Slowly, we made our way toward the church. Our house faded in the distance. Soon, I could see it no more.

"Grandma, is God going to feed my pet pig?" I asked. "Is He going to take care of all the animals? When will we come back home, Grandma?"

She did not answer but kept on rocking Susanna, pleading with God to help us. We joined the long line of wagons in the churchyard. The air filled with a sense of urgency. My eyes were glued to my mother's face. Fear was the only thing I saw. People darted around connecting with their family members and friends. Others huddled in small groups next to their wagons. I wondered what was happening. Every once in a while I caught the word "Russe" in the family conversations.

Who were the Russe? What had we done to make them so angry? Would they really kill us? Maybe if I just behaved and kept as quiet as possible. Grandmother could take care of Susanna and everything would work out. ... I was five years old.

So, we began our long trek westward with more than 500 wagons stretching more than six kilometers (3.7 miles). Evacuees packed the road in both directions as far as the eye could see. We tried taking alternate, less congested roads, and some days we fell behind by 30 kilometers (18.6 miles) as a consequence.

The authorities tried to enforce strict discipline and insisted we keep wagons in line. People with horses were upset because wagons with oxen slowed them down. We traveled from one train station to the next, encountering a multitude of people at each station. It soon became apparent that our wagons would be our only mode of transportation.

During the day, our wagons were spaced far enough apart so planes did not mistake them for a train. Trains were often bombed to prevent supplies from getting to the German Army. We held our breath as we watched the bombers carry their loads overhead. I soon learned that the glistening silver planes were American, while the dark-colored planes were Russian. This was the only way we were able to identify who was trying to kill us on any given day.

Only once did a fighter plane deliberately attack our wagon train. Several wagons were damaged and two children sustained minor injuries. After quickly repairing the damaged wagons, we continued without delaying the others. At night, we camped outside the nearest city and formed circles with our wagons while the animals grazed in the nearby fields. Fires or lights of any kind were strictly forbidden for fear of being targeted.

Only a few weeks into our journey, Uncle Alzner's son Valentine suddenly became seriously ill. As a physician, he assessed the situation and decided he had no choice but to return home to care for his son. He did not want to put both of his sons at risk, so he insisted that his second son, Bernard, continue with our group as we kept heading west. They didn't know at the time, but they wouldn't see each other again for decades.

Slowly, the wagon train snaked along the Danube toward Germany. Some wondered if our ancestors had traveled the same route in reverse, from the Moselle-Rhine area to Botsch, Romania. Now, more than eight hundred years later, we were heading back. My mother walked the 1,500 kilometers (932 miles) to Salzburg, Austria. At night, Mother slept under the wagon while my grandmother, my sister, and I cuddled inside to keep warm.

Everyone pitched in when one of the wagons broke down or an animal had to be put down because of illness or injury. No one was left behind. There were three burials along the way.

At the Austrian border, the wagon train came to an abrupt halt. Austria was annexed in 1938 and was now considered a part of Greater Germany. The Austrian authorities denied us entry and told us to turn back. Turning back, however, was not an option. Heading into the "welcoming arms" of the Red Army was not an option. We ignored their order and decided to bide our time, living in the open fields in our wagons. Days turned into weeks while we waited for permission to continue our trek.

Meanwhile, my mother saw to it that we had enough food to eat and the animals had the necessary care. Sometimes the German military brought food, sometimes they did not. Every evening we prayed that my father and Uncle George were safe and that my father would bring good news when he caught up with us.

Eight grueling weeks passed since we left home. Finally, the waiting and negotiations ended. On November 8, 1944, after all our animals were vaccinated, we were allowed to continue through Wiener-Neüstadt near Vienna, on to St. Pölten, and finally to Wolfsgraben, approximately 41 kilometers (25.4 miles) west of Vienna.

The weather turned bitter cold. The bombings increased. The next few months were terrifying. Vienna, as well as nearby towns, were constantly bombed because of the oil production facilities in the area. Anti-aircraft gun blockhouses surrounded the city.

Here, the authorities organized us into small groups. An Austrian family, whose house resembled a fairytale castle, would be our host. The house, built entirely of stone and sitting high on a hill overlooking a huge forest, was imposing.

From this vantage point, we watched as the bombers flew above the forest toward their targets. As long as they were not coming straight at us, there was nothing to fear. Occasionally, a plane went down into the trees in flames.

I dreaded the sound of the wailing sirens and the look on my mother's face. Her fear seemed to transfer into my body. As soon as the sirens went off, we ran into the bomb shelter built into the hillside. When there was not enough time to make it to the bomb shelter, we hid under the bed and prayed. The windows shattered on more than one occasion.

The weeks dragged on, the bombings continued, and so did our ever-present fear that if the bombs did not find us, the Russians surely would. While we were struggling to survive, reports from the Western Front were equally desperate. The Battle of the Bulge, Ardennes Offensive, from December 16, 1944, to Jan 25, 1945, was signaling defeat. Although the U.S. had sustained heavy losses during the first three days of the battle, they would soon regroup.

Our time was running out. The last of the German reserves were now gone. The Luftwaffe had been broken. On the Western Front, the Allies pushed the German Army east, while the Red Army on the Eastern Front was relentless and forced us to flee west. The end was near.

Back home, while we had barely escaped ahead of the Russian troops, a similar evacuation failed in Southern Transylvania. Russian troops overran and occupied that area. All citizens of Germanic descent were apprehended in January of 1945. Approximately 30,000 Transylvanian Saxons were deported to labor camps in Siberia and Central Asia to help rebuild the Soviet Union. Approximately one third perished dreadfully.

Many slaved in the coal mines of Russia until 1952. A good number were not returned to their homeland, but rather shipped to the Russian-occupied Germany. They were separated from their families for years and decades behind the so-called Iron Curtain. Uncle Alzner, along with his second wife, his son Valentine, and his two stepdaughters were among those held captive by the Romanian State.

By March 30,1945, the Russians had crossed the border between Hungary and Austria, and on April 2, they approached from the south and overran Wiener-Neüstadt outside of Vienna. Most Botschers had already unloaded their possessions from their wagons thinking they were staying for a time. However, this was not to be.

We got word just how swiftly the Russians were advancing. From out of nowhere, my father appeared on his horse. We had not seen or heard from him in weeks.

"What are you doing here?" he shouted frantically. "Why did you stop here? I was hoping you would be farther west. You have to leave or you'll be trapped!" he cried. "You cannot stay here. The Russians are almost to Vienna. You have to leave! You have to leave immediately! There is no time to pack anything! Leave *now*!" He disappeared as quickly as he had appeared without getting off his horse and rode on to warn as many as possible.

We abandoned the house on the hill along with our few remaining possessions. There was no time to contact other families. Each family was on their own. Everyone scattered toward other cities and towns, while the distant explosions and gunfire kept coming closer. The Russians attacked Vienna at all entrances to the city. Here, some of our families became separated.

2. THE WAR YEARS

Approximately 50 Botscher families managed to reorganize under the leadership of Reverend Johann Hartig. The former wagon train leader had abandoned us. None of the towns would accept refugees. Some of the families decided to continue toward Linz and the German border. The sick and elderly stopped near Salzburg.

My sister was running a fever. Grandmother was taking care of her as best she could. There was no medicine. Mother had lost a lot of weight. She felt weak and exhausted, and could not continue.

In Salzburg, we appealed to Reverend Cruse, a Lutheran minister at the local church. He agreed to try to help us. The two ministers, Reverend Hartig and Reverend Cruse, negotiated with the mayor of Anthering-Acharting, a small town a few kilometers north of Salzburg. He finally agreed to let this group of Botschers into his town.

The mayor was under the notion that we would only be staying a few days. Each farmer took one family. A few days later, those wagons that had continued returned. No other town would accept them, so they rejoined our group in Anthering.

**Our one-room cottage on the Austrian farm in Anthering
Taken 54 yrs. later, 1999, on my first trip back there.
The hardy-stemmed weeds I wove into baskets were still growing there.**

3. THE AUSTRIAN COTTAGE

All Austrian homesteads in this rural area had a small second house near the main manor resembling a mother-in-law cottage. Each Botscher family ended up in one of these small one-room cottages. Saxons outnumbered the residents in the small town.

When the Austrians first saw us, they thought we were gypsies and hid in their houses in fear. Our Quaker-like dress was unnerving. They were overwhelmed and terrified by the sheer number of strange-looking people swarming into their quiet town.

Weeks later, we were still there with nowhere else to go. The farmers weren't happy, and we could not really blame them. Their small country with a population of approximately 800,000 people swelled to over 2,000,000 with all the refugees. For the time being, we were stuck with each other.

While a number of our Botscher families managed to cling together, other families were scattered in all directions. Some could not find their family members or relatives and didn't know whether they were dead or alive. There was no way to find out what happened to them. Had the Russians caught them—executed or deported them—or were they injured and hiding somewhere? Some families would never get answers.

Wearily, we unpacked the few suitcases we had hastily grabbed. Not much was left. On the Anthering farm, the bombing was not as intense as near Vienna. Daily, we struggled to survive in "our" little cottage on the Austrian farm.

3. THE AUSTRIAN COTTAGE

The cottage consisted of one room approximately 14 by 14 feet. Upon entering, to the left of the door stood a wood burning stove that extended nearly to the corner. Two beds almost touching, took up the whole right side of the room, wall to wall. A long rectangular wooden table, with an equally long bench, under a window occupied the remaining corner. There were also a couple of chairs we moved around to where needed. We cooked, ate, and slept in that room. Outhouses were still in vogue, the same as back home.

In exchange for food and a place to sleep, Mother agreed to work on the farm while Grandmother Gramelt took care of my sister and me. The farmer had a large herd of cows that needed milking twice a day along with the other endless farm chores. My mother worked long hours for one egg. At the end of the day, we were still unwanted intruders.

During the first few months, the farmer and his wife provided our main meal because we had no food. The meal consisted of schmarn and soup. Schmarn was made of flour mixed with water and fried in lard until it had the appearance of cut-up pancakes. Sprinkled with sugar, schmarn became a daily staple for us. The soup was served in a large communal bowl and placed in the center of the table. Usually we were no fewer than ten people.

Everyone reached into the common bowl with a spoon. Sometimes, by the time the spoon reached my mouth, little was left. I was crazy about the schmarn and could not get enough of it.

Mother was sick a lot of the time. When she was not working for the farmer, she stayed in bed. Grandmother took care of her when she cried.

Here, for the first time, I witnessed my mother's uncontrollable shivering. Her body shook from head to toe and I could hear her teeth chattering between her sobs. Grandmother heated bricks on the stove, wrapped them in rags, and I helped put them in Mother's bed to warm her body.

Grandmother wrapped baked onions in cheesecloth and applied them to the festering boils Mother had developed on her body. Although I tried hard to be useful, there wasn't much I could do, and I often felt like a burden. Grandmother kept repeating, "God help us, God help us." I did not join her. Instead, I kept watching for some sign that God was helping us. He did not and things only got worse.

Everything and everyone became infested with fleas. We searched for them in their favorite hiding places, in the seams of bed sheets and clothing. Then we boiled everything, but some always managed to escape.

To make matters worse, I contracted head lice. Mother spent hours looking through my hair. She had a super-fine comb which worked by pulling the attached nits away from the hair. Mostly it was search-and-destroy, one louse at a time. My mother placed either the louse or the nit on a mirror and squashed each with her thumbnail until you could hear a *pop*. She could not get rid of all of them.

Somehow, she got her hands on gasoline and saturated my head, thinking that would kill them. My scalp began to peel. It burned so bad, I forgot about the lice.

From the Russian Front came word that three of our Botscher men had been shot. Two men were dead. The third was badly injured but survived.

Uncle George was the survivor, but he lost his right leg from above the knee. Several weeks later, he managed to join us in Anthering. I watched as he limped over to the nearest chair, throwing his leg forward with his hip. With a matter-of-fact attitude, he took off his shiny new wooden leg and demonstrated how the hinge bent the knee and how the leg attached.

Uncle George's wound looked red and was still healing. Grandmother did not say anything. Quietly, she moved next

3. THE AUSTRIAN COTTAGE

to him, gently placing her hand on what was left of his leg. He was alive! That was all that mattered to her.

The news from the German Front kept getting more and more desperate. My father somehow managed to elude both the American bombs and the Russian soldiers. Silently, one night while we were sleeping, he joined us in the cottage.

When I awoke the following morning, my father was in the middle of a heated discussion with Uncle George. Mother and Grandmother were sitting at the table listening intently. My sister was still sleeping.

As soon as I joined them, the tone of the conversation changed. According to my father, the Russians were now controlling Vienna. Uncle George and Father talked incessantly about the fighting, their Botscher comrades, friends injured or killed, and the deteriorating state of the German Army. They expected Russians to show up at the door any day. *What were their plans when they found us?* Any time they caught me listening to their conversation, they immediately switched to another language.

What was so bad that they didn't want me to know?

My mind conjured up all sorts of dreadful scenarios. So far, the two men had avoided capture, and for that, we were all grateful—but what if the Russians did show up?

My father's reaction to the bombing was the exact opposite of my mother's. While my mother was in a constant state of panic, Father exuded calm. He strolled leisurely along the hillside in the open field, watching the bombers deliver their loads. Nothing rattled him. He seemed fearless. Unless Mother insisted, he did not join us in the bomb shelter.

Meanwhile, in Anthering, despite that long awful winter, spring arrived and the hills and fields turned a lush green.

4. WORLD WAR II ENDS

Standing near the road in front of the cottage, I spotted a truck filled with soldiers speeding toward me. I was terrified. We had just survived an intense bombing three days earlier. Now these soldiers found us. All the horror stories I heard came to life in my mind. Certain they were going to shoot me, I ran back toward the cottage, screaming frantically, "They're here, they're here! Hide, hide!"

"Where can I hide?" There was no place to hide.

The truck drove by without stopping. It was only a matter of time before they returned. "They're Americans!" my grandmother called out.

Was that supposed to calm us?

My mother seemed relieved, more than likely because of the horrific stories of Russian soldiers torturing ethnic Germans which I overheard when they thought I wasn't listening. Mother decided that if we were going to be killed, it was better to be killed by Americans than by Russians. She was much more terrified of Russians.

It didn't make sense to me, so I was quiet, watched, and listened.

American tanks rolled through Salzburg in May of 1945. The bombing stopped. The war was over. No more running, no more hiding. Nine months had passed since we left home. Miraculously, we were still alive and together as a family. There was no time to worry about what had happened to our homestead and our animals or even when and if we could return. We thanked God and counted our blessings. We were alive and Salzburg was occupied by Americans.

Grandmother began practicing her English. She had not used it in decades. It was just a matter of time before she would need it to communicate with the American soldiers.

U.S. Armed Forces controlled the provinces of Salzburg and Upper Austria (south of the Danube River) and parts of the Austrian capital, Vienna. Parts of Vienna became Russian-occupied. Of those who found themselves in Russian-occupied zones in Austria, 8,000 were forcibly returned to Transylvania. Had we stayed in Wolfsgraben near Vienna, the Red Army would have apprehended us. Our destiny changed by fleeing a mere three hours further west to Anthering, a few kilometers north of Salzburg.

Three American soldiers paid us a "visit" a few days later. My father and Uncle George disappeared. The soldiers checked us out and looked around the cottage. There were no signs of men staying in the cottage.

My mother and I sat quietly on the bed. My heart was pounding and I was sure they could hear it. However, the soldiers barely noticed us. Grandmother Gramelt was doing all the talking. I could not understand a word they were saying. It seemed like an eternity before they left.

Without shooting us, they headed toward the main manor. We did not see Uncle George or my father until the following day. When they rejoined us, everyone switched and spoke Romanian. It really upset me. When I asked what they were saying, they would invariably tell me something positive in order to stifle my questions.

I did not believe them for a minute but there was nothing I could do about it.

German soldiers were apprehended daily all around us. Courageously, Grandmother grabbed two abandoned horses while their German owners disappeared into the nearby swamp where heavy reeds could hide them for a while. She wished the soldiers well as she quickly led the horses toward the farmer's barn so as not to draw attention to them.

The farmer provided regular clothing for my father and Uncle George so they could blend in with the locals. After a while, the Americans stopped looking for German soldiers.

Uncle George was very handy, and like his father, he too was a jack of all trades. In many ways, he was more attentive to my sister and me than our own father.

He immediately decided to raise rabbits to help feed us and began building cages. Our great expectations faded when rats ate the first batch. Then, he built stronger cages. The rats always seemed to find ways of bypassing his ingenious barriers. This infuriated Uncle George because each rabbit the rats ate meant one less meal for us.

In the evenings, we sat and listened to my father and Uncle George recount horror stories of atrocities committed against women and children by Russian soldiers. In my imagination, I could actually see these women and children and feel their pain. It was difficult to stop thinking about the woman with her breasts nailed to the table or the decapitated children thrown on heaps. I was afraid of everything, always expecting horrible things to happen to me at any moment.

My fear eventually turned into intense hatred for anything having to do with war. Like Uncle George and my father, I eventually came to the same conclusion—politicians were responsible for wars while civilians paid the price for their folly. Both Mother and Grandmother were especially grateful to have both men with us. ...We were so far from home, and without hope of returning.

I picked snowdrops for Mother in early spring. Later I picked the African violets that grew behind the cottage, and I foraged for forget-me-nots, my favorite. Chamomile flowers grew between the railroad tracks behind the cottage. Mother dried the flowers and made tea for us. She taught me how to knit socks and weave baskets from the hardy stemmed weeds growing abundantly in the field next to the cottage. I did not want to add to Mother's already overwhelming worries so I worked hard at becoming this perfect little person. Regardless of how well-behaved I was, I could not make my mother happy.

**1946 Maria, Herman, Susanna
Herman - Our Austrian
childhood playmate**

**Susanna, Johnny, Maria
With one of our meals**

5. LIFE IN THE AUSTRIAN COTTAGE

Uncle George's wooden leg did not restrict him from hard work, and he constantly looked out for our well-being. The following spring, he planted a vegetable garden with potatoes, lettuce, radishes, cucumbers, carrots, tomatoes, and lots of cabbage. He filled a large barrel with cabbage, then poured brine over it and let the whole thing ferment. We ate pickled cabbage all year long.

The rats got fewer of our rabbits. I don't know what Uncle George fed them but they became huge. Most of them were gray, cuddly, and very tame. They were so fat they could hardly run. Susanna and I played with them before they became our meal. Uncle George never let us see him slaughter them. They tasted delicious!

That summer while playing, I lost my grip on a tree branch and fell into a puddle. When I came back in the house, Mother gave me a painful spanking because my dress was all muddy. My wrist was swollen and ached.

Cousin Bernie put me on the handlebars of his bike and we headed for the hospital in Salzburg. While trying to cross the street, another biker ran into us and knocked me off the bike. I fell to the ground and sustained a gash on my forehead. I used my left hand to keep the blood from running into my eye while my right hand ached and was useless. There was no way to hold on to the handlebars on the bike so we walked the rest of the way to the hospital.

When the doctor told me my arm was broken, I was afraid. No one in our family had ever broken anything before.

5. LIFE IN THE AUSTRIAN COTTAGE

The cast he put on my arm extended from my fingers all the way to my elbow. After the doctor bandaged my forehead, we left the hospital and headed back. It took forever to get home. Mother did not say anything to me, and I spent the next two months babying my right arm and feeling sorry for myself.

Aunt Rosi and Uncle John lived in Windsor, Ontario. They asked their friend Arthur, a Canadian soldier stationed in Salzburg, to look in on their three children—cousins John, George, and Maria—who lived near our cottage. I couldn't stop staring at Arthur in his uniform. At six years old, I think I fell in love for the first time. Arthur was such a great help to us. I always looked forward to his visits with my cousins.

Cousin Maria was my second mother without the spankings, always gentle and kind. Whenever possible, I stayed at her place overnight. She loved when I warmed her feet. For some reason her feet were always ice cold.

Between Arthur and Grandmother's conversations with the regularly "visiting" American soldiers, we learned about the help available to us. We applied for and began receiving much-needed and appreciated CARE packages.

The CARE packages contained things we had never seen or eaten before. We all liked the cans of Spam included in every package. I had never tasted a chocolate bar or chewing gum.

At first, my sister and I thought the chewing gum was candy, and we both ended up swallowing the gum. It wasn't until one of the soldiers noticed me swallowing the gum that he showed me how to chew it and told me never to swallow it but rather to spit it out. After several failures, I finally remembered to spit it out. My sister and I enjoyed the chocolate bars, but the gum lost its flavor quickly, and it seemed a bit silly to keep chewing something without any flavor.

During one of these American soldier's visits, I noticed a very dark-skinned soldier, and I wondered why he was so dirty. Why hadn't he washed? Regardless of how many times

Mother explained to me that he was born with dark skin and no amount of washing could change the color, I was not totally convinced.

During the fall, Mother became pregnant again. She was not happy about having another mouth to feed, and the news put even more stress on her.

Weeks turned into months. Months turned into seasons. We were grateful our family lived on a farm where we could provide food for ourselves. Displaced people in the cities were not as fortunate and food for them was scarce.

Innovative Uncle George got his hands on sheets of aluminum from a downed airplane. He created beautiful aluminum bracelets with elaborate engravings. When possible he sold them to help feed and clothe us. Mother fashioned hand-sewn blouses for Susanna and me out of parachute fabric Uncle George found in the field.

My new baby brother was born the following summer, July, 1946, in Seekirchen, one of the Salzburg districts. They named him Johann after my father, as was the custom.

During the following months, Mother continued crying almost every time she nursed him. I did not think she would ever stop crying. When Mother talked about the pain during childbirth, I listened closely. My stomach hurt as I pictured her in agony, and I could never understand what "cutting the cord" meant. My family all laughed at me when I declared that I was never going to have children because it was such a horrible, cruel, scary world. I was seven years old.

There were many firsts during that time in my life. When my toothache persisted, Uncle George decided to take me to a dentist. This was my first visit to a dentist. I was terrified, recalling memories of the doctor in the white coat who treated me when I broke my arm. To me, the sight of a white coat meant pain. I climbed up on the chair, not knowing what to expect. No one said a word. Uncle George

5. LIFE IN THE AUSTRIAN COTTAGE

leaned against the wall watching me. I held my breath as the dentist put several shiny pointy instruments on a tray next to me. Then he took one of them and held it over an open flame.

Suddenly, panic set in. No way was I going to let him cut into me with that thing. I jumped out of the chair so fast it caught Uncle George off guard. As I dashed past him, he was not quick enough to grab me before I ran out of the office and down the street. I kept on running without looking back while Uncle George yelled for me to stop. With his wooden leg, he was no match for me. I made it home ahead of him. He was quite upset but he did not force me to go back, and he didn't give me a spanking. For that, I was grateful.

Two of Mother's friends, Grete Fuhrmann and Gustav Hartig, organized a school for the Botscher children in Anthering. I walked to school every day and loved learning. For Mother's Day, the teacher asked me to read a poem in front of the class. The words were so sad and poignant, I began to cry. To my embarrassment, I could not finish and had to sit down.

Meanwhile, life in our little Austrian cottage turned to new problems. We had survived the guns and bombs, now we had to survive the routine of life. At times, our original four inhabitants mushroomed to nine, ten, or eleven with all the uncles and cousins. We slept three and four to a bed. Since there were only two beds in our one-room cottage, some of the adults must have slept in the farmer's barn or wherever else they could find a spot.

What were we going to do?
Where were we going to live?
How were we going to make a living as a family, extended family, and our entire Botscher village?
Austria was not our home. We did not belong here.

The farmers did not relish the thought of having permanent guests on their homesteads. They were anxious to reclaim their property and return to their former way of life without Saxons everywhere.

The only thing we knew for sure was that we could not go home. Life as we had known it was gone. Our homes, our homeland, our identity, our customs, and our traditions were gone forever.

Where did we belong?

Where could we go to survive as a family?

Sobieski – The ship that brought us to Halifax, Nova Scotia

6. EMIGRATING FROM AUSTRIA

As soon as the war ended, my cousins John, George, and Maria's plans began taking shape. Their parents, Aunt Rosi and Uncle John, living in Windsor, immediately began filing the necessary papers for them to immigrate to Canada. Their parents had traveled to Canada from Botsch to work and save their money, just as my grandparents had done earlier in the United States. For years, the war trapped their children in Transylvania and separated them from their parents. The three survived the war with us and now looked forward to becoming a family again.

Together our family decided to apply for entry into the United States. Our final destination was Columbus, Ohio, where Uncle John, the American son, now lived. With the large Saxon population in that region and even distant relatives, we knew they would welcome us. My parents applied for entry to the United States for our family. Grandmother and Uncle George applied separately.

American law allowed entry to the United States to U.S.-born residents in foreign countries and any of their children born before 1940. This meant that my mother and I could emigrate from Austria, but my father and my sister and brother were denied entry. Uncle George, despite having been born in the U.S., was also denied entry. My sister and brother were denied because they were born after 1940. My father and Uncle George were denied because they had served in the German Army. The fact that they did not volunteer for that service or have a choice was irrelevant.

Mother refused to split the family up and chose instead to apply for entry to Canada. Aunt Rosi and Uncle John agreed to sponsor us. Grandmother proceeded with her plans to join her American son, John, in Columbus, while leaving her German son, George, behind in Anthering for the time being.

Months went by after my cousins left for Canada. We continued filling out papers as the days dragged on. Finally, we received a Certificate of Identity. It stated, "This certificate is issued to refugees not enjoying in law or in fact the 'protection' of any government, with the approval of the American Section of the Allied Commission for Austria, through the International Refugee Organization. Its purpose is to serve as a temporary certificate pending the adoption of an international travel document. In no way does it affect the nationality of the bearer."

The papers were stamped with a large DISPLACED PERSONS. On the UNDP Identification Card Nr.7841, someone typed in "peasant" next to the field for occupation. Subsequently, we were referred to as DPs or refugees. These names followed me for many years. Even in school when kids did not call me a "kraut" or "Nazi," they referred to me as a DP or refugee. I hated those labels and the shame I felt when I heard those words.

We spent several days in a refugee camp before boarding the ship for Canada. Our ship was named *Sobieski*. It was huge! I had never seen a ship before much less lived on one for such a long time. I spent my days picking up tossed cigarette butts on the ship's deck for my father. He unwrapped the already-smoked cigarette, emptied what little tobacco was left, rolled it in cigarette paper, and smoked it. Mother spent her days taking care of Susanna and my little brother.

On July 10, 1948, we arrived in Halifax, Nova Scotia. Then we boarded a train to Windsor, Ontario, to join Aunt

6. EMIGRATING FROM AUSTRIA

Rosi and Uncle John and my three cousins who had arrived months ahead of us.

Aunt Rosi and Uncle John fawned over my brother and immediately renamed him Johnny. There undoubtedly were too many Johanns in the family who now all became Johns here in Canada. We all spoke Saxon with my aunt, uncle, and cousins, so names were not a problem. Each person had a nickname in Saxon. However, now we had to identify which John we were talking about in English. We had three generations of names passed down consisting of John, George, Maria, and Susanna.

Johnny had a nice ring to it. I liked his new name. Mine remained Maria in English and Minisha in Saxon, Minisha being the diminutive term for Maria.

Our family enjoyed my aunt's duplex after years of the crowded living conditions in our one-room Austrian cottage. My aunt did not have an outhouse. None of the homes in Windsor had outhouses. What a change! Flushing the toilet was amazing.

My cousin George took me to the nearby park when he wasn't working. Of course, I had never been to a park, and I couldn't help but notice how different my clothes were from the other girls. This became even more apparent one day when I went outside to play with the girl next door.

I immediately felt out of place with my blonde braids and my brown high-top shoes. It didn't help that I couldn't speak a word of English. I had no way of communicating with her. She took one look at me and ran back into her house.

A few weeks later, I stood in front of Aunt Rosi's house waiting for the neighbor girl to come out and play. Glancing up at the sky, I noticed a lot of white smoke trailing from a plane and instantly froze. My teeth clenched, my hair stood on end, and goose bumps covered my body. For a moment, I could not move as I kept my eyes fixed on that plane.

Had the war started again?
Were there bombs in this country, too?
Were they following us?

There was no sound of a siren. I whirled around and charged into the house. It took Aunt Rosi a long time to calm me. She explained the plane was skywriting—something about advertising—which I did not understand.

She kept repeating, "There is no war here and there are no bombs falling." I wanted desperately to believe her, but the fear would not leave me.

Was she really telling me the truth?
How could I be sure?

Our family lived with Aunt Rosi for several months, but we could not get too comfortable or settle in for very long. The Canadian government exacted a price for the privilege of allowing us into their country. Canada had a shortage of farm laborers at the time. In order to gain entry to Canada, even with Aunt Rosi sponsoring us, my mother and father had to agree to spend a year as farm laborers. We had no choice but to fulfill that obligation.

Johnny was two years old. Aunt Rosi and Uncle John were crazy about him. They enjoyed caring for him and took him everywhere. They "adopted" him for that whole year, and he stayed with them while the rest of our family left Windsor to live on a farm. This made it possible for my parents to work full time.

When the time came, my aunt and uncle drove us out to Rodney, a rural town about 60 miles north of Windsor to look for work and a place to live. We met a wonderful Hungarian farmer who needed workers for his tobacco farm. His family spoke only Hungarian among family members. They were all so kind to us. Not only did they hire both of my parents, but they also helped our family find a small frame house to live in.

Although my parents did not speak Hungarian, the language had a familiar ring to it. They had often heard the language spoken back home in Transylvania. Over the next year, my parents learned a little bit of English and a lot of Hungarian. They heard the language spoken every day all day long working alongside this Hungarian family processing the tobacco. They still needed to improve their English, but added to Saxon, German, Romanian, and now Hungarian, they eventually spoke five languages with only an eighth grade education.

My father discovered country music, and in spite of not understanding a single word, he loved listening to it. Country music seemed to touch his very soul, especially Hank Williams songs.

Susanna and I attended a one-room schoolhouse not far from where we lived and began learning English. Starting the first day, the teacher referred to my sister as Susan, and from then on, that became her new name.

My parents bought dozens and dozens of chicks and raised them for food. Chickens, we discovered, were much easier to raise than the rabbits back in Anthering.

I was in charge of feeding them. Later, when they were fully grown, I chased the largest chicken down and held it tightly. Then I stepped on its wings with my foot, at the same time stretching the neck with my left hand while cutting off its head with my right hand. Sometimes a chicken flapped its wings so violently, I lost my grip, and the chicken ran around the pen without its head.

Next came soaking the chicken in hot water, plucking the feathers, and cleaning the body cavity. After taking great care not to cut through the gallbladder, I cut the chicken into pieces, seasoned it with salt, pepper, paprika, and garlic, then baked it for approximately one hour. To test whether or not the chicken was fully cooked, I stuck a fork into the stomach. When the stomach was tender enough for the fork to insert easily, it meant the chicken was done.

We ate chicken daily for that whole year. I was almost ten years old when we returned to Windsor after fulfilling our obligation to the Canadian government.

Maria, Mom, Uncle John, Susan and Johnny on Bike – Rodney Farm 1949

Uncle John visiting from Ohio and bringing Johnny from Windsor to visit us

7. THE REFUGEE IN CANADA

The money my parents made during that year on the tobacco farm did not stretch far enough for both the down payment on the two-bedroom, one-bathroom house and the repayment of the loan to my aunt and uncle. Aunt Rosi and Uncle John wanted their money for our ocean voyage from Austria. So, they introduced my parents to the Beneficial Finance Company in Windsor.

I watched as my parents struggled to repay this loan. They didn't understand why the principal never seemed to go down, regardless of how many payments they made. It was a lifelong lesson for me. I was determined that no Beneficial Finance Company would ever own me.

Down the street a few blocks from our house was the intersection of Giles and Parent. Prince Edward Elementary School was on one corner. The Evangelical Lutheran Church we attended every Sunday was on the corner across from the school. Situated on the third corner was W.D. Lowe Vocational School, which we attended after Prince Edward. Giles and Parent in Windsor remained an important intersection in our family's lives.

Before Susan and I were allowed to attend classes in Prince Edward, the school nurse administered a tuberculosis (TB) skin test on us. My results came back positive, and I had to get a chest X-ray. The X-ray must have turned out okay because they allowed me to attend classes. The nurse instructed me not to take another skin test. She explained that once a person tests positive, it remained positive throughout their life.

Years later, I wondered if my grandfather died of TB instead of asthma and if I was exposed during the time prior to his death.

Susan and I quickly learned English. When Mother and Father spoke Saxon to us, we answered in English. I spent my time on schoolwork and helping Mother, determined not only to be a good student but also to be the top student in my class.

Because I worked so hard at being this dutiful little soldier, it was particularly hurtful when my fourth grade homeroom teacher, Mr. McArthur, accused me of not raising my hand when he was taking attendance. Even though I assured him that I had raised my hand, he did not believe me.

To my embarrassment, he ordered me to stand in the hall outside the classroom. He was angry. Because I was such an obedient student, no teacher had ever punished me. I felt ashamed and hurt. The longer I was out there, the more humiliated and hurt I felt.

Finally, I couldn't bear it any longer. Tears streaming down my face, I walked out of the school building and home to implore my mother for help. Mother would tell Mr. McArthur that I had not lied to him. If I said that I had raised my hand, he should believe me. I would never deliberately do anything to upset him. She knew me.

That evening when Mother came home from work, I told her what had happened. She listened attentively but was not very supportive. Mother felt I should have obeyed Mr. McArthur. After all, he was the teacher and the final authority. Not only did she not support me, she told me that it was not possible for her to come to school with me the next day because she needed to go to work. I felt crushed and betrayed.

The following day, I walked back into the classroom by myself. As soon as Mr. McArthur spotted me, he told me to wait in the next room. Out of the corner of my eye, I saw him

7. THE REFUGEE IN CANADA

reach for the leather strap in his drawer. He did not want to hear anything I had to say. Towering above me, he barked, "Hold out your hand."

My first instinct was to run. If only there was some place to run. But where? It felt as though I was delivering myself up willingly for execution, for a crime I did not commit. I held out my right hand, then my left, then my right, then my left. When was he going to stop? You could hear the crack of the strap echoing all the way down the long hallway. The whole class heard my sobs. He paused for a moment. With a smirk on his face, he looked down at me and ordered me to kneel.

I desperately wanted it to end. Maybe if I kneeled in front of him, he would stop. However, how could I kneel? He was punishing me for something I did not do. Not only did he want to hurt me physically, he wanted to break me spiritually. What did he have against krauts, refugees, or DPs? Why did this teacher hate me so much?

Kneeling on command in front of him was the ultimate humiliation. I couldn't do it, regardless of what he did to me. I was not going to kneel. Looking up through my tears, I fiercely met his gaze, clenched my teeth, and replied, "Never!"

He smiled, apparently getting the reaction he wanted. "Hold out your hand," he repeated. Seemingly gleeful, he continued with yet another round of strapping. Not only was I falsely accused and unjustly punished by Mr. McArthur, but totally *abandoned* and left to fend for myself by my mother. I didn't know which hurt more. The injustice of it all was overwhelming. There was no one in the whole world to protect me.

Where was this God that my family kept praying to? He too had forsaken me and never made a move to help me. As far back as I could remember, He never helped me with anything.

Why not? Surely, HE knew I was innocent. There was no help from anyone. I felt totally alone and abandoned.

By contrast, my science teacher, Mr. Hill, was the complete opposite of Mr. McArthur. I loved being in his class. Apparently, he felt no animosity toward refugees, krauts, or DPs. Mr. Hill inspired curiosity and made learning exciting. Science was my favorite subject, and I could not get enough. There was never a dull moment in his class and so much to learn from him. How could anyone know so much about so many things? I couldn't wait to get to his class, and I hung on to his every word.

Mr. Hill was very strict but fair. Tall and skinny, you could see his bones protrude through his shirt at the shoulders. He addressed the class peering over the top of his round wire-rimmed glasses. When we studied the human body, he chose my drawing of the heart while instructing the class. According to my sister who was in his class two years later, he used my drawing even after I left Prince Edward.

The miniature model of our sun and the surrounding planets on his desk intrigued me. He once told the class, "With as many planets as there are in the galaxy, why should Earth be the only planet with life on it?"

The class debated that for a while and everyone shared their views. It made perfect sense to me and I agreed. How could anyone doubt Mr. Hill? From that moment on, I was certain there was life on other planets.

I wondered how long it would be before I would meet someone from another planet?

Then there was his foolproof method for curing hiccups. Anyone in his class lucky enough to have hiccups was privy to his treatment. All must have been sworn to secrecy because no

7. THE REFUGEE IN CANADA

one ever divulged his secret. Mr. Hill would usher his student to his plant room adjoining the classroom. You could hear a pin drop in the classroom while we waited, wondered, and speculated as to what he was doing. What was his marvelous method for curing hiccups? After about five minutes, the student returned to the class, smiling and cured of hiccups.

Several years went by with me desperately hoping that I would get hiccups in his class. Regretfully, I graduated from Prince Edward without ever learning his secret. Mr. Hill was by far my favorite and most admired teacher. He helped make up for Mr. McArthur, whom I considered mentally unbalanced.

When my father became a little more fluent in English, he quit his job at the foundry and got a better job at Chrysler. At least there, he could breathe more easily. Things were looking up. With his higher salary, there was renewed hope of paying off the bills. My parents' hopes, however, were short-lived. The following year Father was laid off from his new job and unable to find work anywhere. My parents were constantly arguing over money or the lack thereof.

Meanwhile, Uncle George was allowed to immigrate to Canada and he joined us in Windsor. Having been refused entry into the United States from Austria, he hoped to gain entry to the U.S. from Canada. He lived with us in Windsor while waiting for his mother, my Grandmother Gramelt, to arrive in Columbus, Ohio. In the meantime, he brushed up on his English, which he had not spoken since he was a child. My relationship with Uncle George was completely different here than in Anthering.

The months he spent with us were horrible times for Mother. The aftermath of the war was beginning to take its toll on Uncle George. He began drinking heavily and used his amputated leg as an excuse. Father, now out of a job, felt equally miserable. In addition to not working, he too was trying to adjust to a new country, a new culture and language, while also suffering from the after-effects of the war. The two spent their days drinking and drowning their sorrows at the local tavern. Johnny spent those days with them, mostly sleeping out of sight under the table at the tavern. That way everyone could pretend he was not there.

Now there were *two* men in the house who did not have jobs or money. Uncle George used his excellent skills to build a whisky still in the basement on Giles. Uncle George and my father got drunk daily without going to the tavern, while Mother kept on slaving away, trying to support the family.

The arguments grew louder and more frequent. Mother was beside herself. When he was drunk, Uncle George became belligerent and yelled. The stress was palpable. Hardly a day went by without arguing.

There was no discipline in the house. Susan did not help me with the housework and spent as much time as possible with her friends away from home. Johnny was still too young. Neither listened to me or took anything I said seriously. Susan and I argued constantly about housework and her pitching in. It was a carbon copy of what our parents were doing. I hated arguing. It was such a waste. As far as I could see, arguing never solved anything. I made a mental note promising myself:

"When I grow up, I'm never going to argue with anyone ever again."

As much as I had adored Uncle George in Anthering, I was beginning to resent him. Father was absolutely no help with the family, and I couldn't understand why he was making Mother so miserable. It seemed he had no consideration for her at all. There was no excuse for him not going out and looking for a job, any kind of job, or pitching in and helping

7. THE REFUGEE IN CANADA

around the house. Mother blamed her brother George for many of their arguments.

When my parents argued, it was a strange kind of one-way arguing. Mother did most of the arguing by herself with Father looking on.

Her main complaint usually included "Hunsi, Hunsi," Saxon for Hans, which is German for Johann, which is John in English.

"How could you do this? How could you do this?" She followed up with, "You have no consideration for me. I can't believe you did such and such."

Mother never waited for him to answer. Even on those rare occasions when he managed to get a word in edgewise, usually in a low voice, Mother continued her ranting. Through all those years of arguing, I never once heard my father raise his voice to my mother. Mostly he watched her pacing back and forth venting. Every once in a while he would shake his head and make a little snapping sound with his tongue, almost as if he wanted her to know he was listening. The fact that he didn't engage her seemed to frustrate her even more. Eventually she exhausted herself and stopped.

At least once a month, my mother threatened to jump off the Ambassador Bridge if father didn't stop drinking and help shoulder some of the responsibilities. This bridge connected Detroit, Michigan, to Windsor, Ontario. Watching and listening to Mother's anguish, I was convinced she was serious and meant to follow through on her threats. *Then, what would happen to us?*

I lay awake late into the night listening for sounds indicating she might be leaving for the bridge. There was not much else she could do except nag, complain, and threaten to kill herself. Arguing and complaining became a habit and a way of life in that house. I could not help but notice that no amount of either made any difference and had absolutely no impact on my father's behavior.

One Saturday, my father decided to turn the tables on Mother. Before Mother began her recitations of the week's complaints and threats, he pretended to poison himself by drinking a bottle of iodine. I guess he wanted to scare her or get her attention—or God only knows why. He did not see me come into the kitchen. I was behind him and watched him empty the bottle of iodine into the kitchen sink before putting it to his mouth. He was upset with me when I told Mother, and their arguing only heated up.

Mother left the house every day at four in the morning for her two-hour long bus ride to work in Detroit. She did not get home until evening. They struggled to make ends meet, while payments to the Beneficial Finance Company continued.

The guilt I felt when asking for a quarter for ice cream or a soft drink usually kept me from asking. At the same time, I resented when Susan and Johnny, seemingly without thinking twice, had no guilt asking for and receiving that quarter. While Mother worked outside the house, I became the workhorse in the house, cleaning, washing, ironing and taking care of Johnny. Instead of ironing her own clothes, Susan sneaked down the basement, took my ironed clothes, and wore them.

Father forged Mother's signature on the $52 monthly check she received for the three of us from the Canadian government. Fifty-two dollars was enough money to feed the family for a couple weeks. However, Father quickly spent it on whatever he wanted. His sense of responsibility for a wife and children was nonexistent.

He was in the military service for many of their early years of marriage. During those years, Mother took care of Susan and me with Grandmother Gramelt's help. My father only visited every few months on leave from the army. He was never involved in taking care of us. I didn't know him,

7. THE REFUGEE IN CANADA

and since Susan was two years younger than I was, she didn't know him either. By the time he joined us in Anthering in the spring of 1945, I was five and a half years old. In Anthering, Uncle George took over the responsibilities of parenting Susan and me. He was the one who saw to it that there was food on the table and that we behaved and were clothed, especially when Mother was sick.

Aunt Rosina, my father's half-sister in Chatham, Ontario, told me that soldiers had raped their mother when they were traveling through our town after World War I. I don't know if this is true. My father's mother was very young when she gave birth to my father. Father's grandmother took care of him as an infant. Later, when his mother married, my father did not live with the couple, but remained with his grandmother.

Whether his mother and stepfather didn't want him or whatever the reason, my father never had a father as a role model. He never learned what a man's responsibilities are to his children and his wife. With no Uncle George or Grandmother Gramelt helping, my father didn't have a clue. The sole responsibility of raising us fell on Mother as well as providing for the family financially. I also pulled an adult load by taking care of the house and Johnny.

While I did everything to please Mother, Susan did everything to irritate her. I was the obedient daughter in order to avoid punishment. Susan, on the other hand, talked back, stayed out late, and even stayed overnight at her friends' houses. Mother would beat her even into her teenage years. I often wondered if Mother and her siblings were physically abused by their parents when they were growing up. She never said and only told me about the axe incident with her father. (Chapter 1, page 3)

I never saw Johnny being hit by either of our parents. Johnny was glued to our father the same way Susan was glued to Grandmother Gramelt in Anthering.

One of my great escapes and joys was spending time in the park away from my family. Lanspeary Park was right across the street from our house. There, I learned to swim and dive in the pool. During the winter months, the park had an ice rink where I learned how to skate with a pair of black skates I found in the alley behind our house. Obviously, someone had received a new pair for Christmas. I painted them white with house paint from our basement. With my winter pants pulled low over them, I pretended they were a Christmas gift and never even considered anyone would notice they were not girls' ice skates.

8. SCRIPTING

Scripting, as used in this book simply means a kind of *programming* by the use of repetition over many years. A parent, by repeating something often enough, may influence a child into accepting that parent's belief as gospel. In my case, my mother did the *scripting* with her never-ending advice. Consequently, for a time, I lived my life according to her belief, almost as if she had handed me the script of a play to follow. ...

Growing up, I don't remember my father ever giving me even the tiniest bit of advice. He barely even spoke to me except through my mother. Mother, on the other hand, never ran out of advice—especially her two favorites, which she repeated throughout my life.

The first, *"Don't depend on a man to pay your rent."* I concluded this was because she could never depend on my father to support the family, so it was left up to her.

The second, *"Don't want so much, Marie. Be satisfied with less."*

Fulfilling her first scripting was easy. I was only 12 when I got my first job waitressing, about a block from where we lived. I decided early in life that skills were much more valuable for earning a living than going to school for the next 20 years. So, I began collecting skills.

I loved waitressing and earning money. Soon I was buying my own clothes and even clothes for my sister and Mother.

In the evening, listening to "The Shadow" on the radio along with "The Squeaking Door" sent shivers down my spine. My imagination soared. Later, my parents bought a 12-inch black and white TV. We were all mesmerized.

Then I opened my first bank account. My largest bank balance was $34. However, the pride, independence, and confidence it gave me were immeasurable. I was rich!

Part of my weekly five or six dollars were spent on clothes. The remainder would go straight into my bank account, and I withdrew a dollar or two whenever I wanted to buy something minor. Never again would I ask either of my parents for a quarter to buy a Coke or 7-Up.

The first time I went into the neighborhood store to purchase a bottle of 7-Up, I asked for *Zup*. The man didn't know what I wanted so I pointed to the bottle.

"Oh," he said laughing. You mean 7-Up?"

"Yes," I answered, embarrassed.

Conveniently, the Tivoli Theatre was right next to the bank. On Saturdays, I paid 25 cents to watch a Hopalong Cassidy or Gene Autry movie. However, my favorites were always the musicals, especially *Show Boat* with Howard Keel and Kathryn Grayson or Mario Lanza in *The Great Caruso*. To me, Mario Lanza was the greatest singer in the whole world.

I enjoyed all that wondrous entertainment for 25 cents. It was a terrific escape from the nonstop arguments and my dysfunctional family. The rest of my life consisted of studying, housework, waitressing and Lanspeary Park.

In the summer when I wasn't swimming in the park, I watched kids play soccer or a fierce game of lacrosse. Lacrosse was very popular and always attracted a large audience. The park also had a greenhouse with beautiful flowers and shrubs. How lucky I felt to have this park so close to my house.

Mother's second scripting, "Don't want so much, Marie. Be satisfied with less," was much more difficult for me. However, I was aware that I didn't like it, especially when it made me feel guilty for wanting more. And, I did want more, *so much more.* There was no end to my wanting. I wanted a normal family that didn't argue, parents who made me feel safe, a father who loved us enough to provide for us, a mother who stopped beating Susan and stopped threatening suicide, a sister who pitched in and did her share of the work, and a brother who would grow up faster and take care of himself and give me a break.

Most of all I wanted to be Canadian, just a happy carefree kid like the other kids on the block. They all seemed so happy without serious problems or responsibilities. There was no relating to them. We may have walked this earth the same number of years, but I was so much older, ancient by comparison, with the weight of the world on my shoulders.

At times, my heart ached with sadness when I realized I could never be one of those carefree kids. I had to live with the memories of constantly running and hiding from people trying to kill me. The ever-present fear, while trying to survive didn't magically disappear in this new country. It seemed to be locked up somewhere in my mind, and destroyed any chance of being a carefree kid. I was old at the age of ten. No amount of wishing could change the facts. I was a Saxon refugee, a kraut, a DP, a foreigner in this country. Would I ever belong here or anywhere? It took many years to learn that it is far more noble to wish and dream than to stifle out desire.

I envied my neighborhood playmates on Giles. All were Catholic. They could do anything they wanted—lie, steal, and cheat. All they had to do was go to confession, say a few Hail Marys, and everything was forgiven. Then they could repeat their bad behavior the following week. As a Lutheran, I didn't go to confession. There was no forgiveness, and as for that reward constantly talked about in church, that was only given after death.

During those years, I was still sitting in church listening to what a rotten sinner I was, even though I never felt like a rotten sinner. According to our minister's teaching, God was an angry, vengeful God. God was to be feared. No thought or act escaped Him regardless of how insignificant. "Keep thee only unto him," would not only help steer me into an abusive marriage but would also keep me from leaving for many years.

Our church service was delivered in German since the majority of the congregation was Saxon. The sermons seemed to be judged by how many people ended up crying. The minister certainly knew which buttons to push, invoking painful memories with references to the "homeland" or "what once was" or stories of how we were driven out of our ancestral homes. These images always brought tearful memories to the congregation. You could hear a whole lot of sniffling going on. Afterward, these same people exclaimed what a wonderful preacher he was and what a great sermon he delivered. Something about that whole scene did not sit right in my gut. I always felt worse coming out of church than before going in.

Mother definitely was afraid of God. She even believed laughing was a sin. Once in an unguarded moment, she found something hilarious enough to burst out laughing. Quickly, she stopped herself, put her hand over her mouth, and mumbled, "God forgive me." It was the only time I heard her laugh aloud.

Between the minister's sermons and Mother's reactions, I was convinced that God was watching us. He was up there somewhere, dishing out reward and punishment.

During heavy thunderstorms, Mother switched from, "God forbid" to "God protect us" or "God help us" in Saxon. I wondered if God really was behind the thunder and lightning. If He was, then He could easily strike me dead at any moment. Like Mother, I desperately feared lightning and thunder. During especially fierce lightning storms, I found myself breaking out in a cold sweat.

8. SCRIPTING

If God was that powerful,

Why didn't He make life a little better for our family?
Why didn't He help my father get a job?
Why didn't He make my responsibilities a bit lighter?
Why did everything have to be so serious?
Would it spoil some grand plan if I were just a little bit happier?

He seemed great at punishing, but there was not much rewarding going on, at least not as far as our family was concerned. I followed every rule, obeyed every demand placed on me, and tried living up to our church's teachings of "Not sinning in thought, word, and deed."

Why was it not working?
Where was my reward for all my hard work?
Where was this God that we constantly prayed to and talked to?
How much more could I do?
Should I try even harder?
Would that make any difference?

Every Saturday, Mother and Father joined their friends at the Saxon Hall. The Saxons had banded together and purchased a building where they could have social gatherings. The first floor resembled a gymnasium with chairs lining the walls. There was an area for a band while the whole floor was for dancing. Everyone danced. Several hundred people would gather every Saturday night to dance and enjoy their fellow Saxons. The lower level consisted of a bar and many tables with chairs.

It was a time in Windsor when Italians would go to their Italian Club, the Polish would go to the Polish Club, and Saxons would go to the Saxon Club. Other ethnic Germans would attend an even larger organization called the Teutonia Club.

My parents felt comfortable among friends who spoke the same language, with similar backgrounds and similar challenges. Father would drink while Mother pleaded with him to stop.

He never stopped. After a while, she gave up and spent her evening commiserating with her friends. Father laughed and danced by himself, snapping his fingers high over his head to the rhythm of the song he sang. He loved singing. Eventually in-between drinks or when the band took a break, his friends would join him in a rousing chorus of one of the many German songs they all knew. These songs seemed to transport them all to a better place of long ago, a place before we all became refugees, without a country, without our homes, without our way of life, without belonging.

Johnny and I were forced to accompany my parents to these dances. Susan ran away and refused to join us, risking yet another beating. After a while, Mother realized that Susan would never listen regardless of how many times she hit her, and the beatings became less frequent. Johnny sat and watched while I had to dance at least one dance with every old fart who asked me. Refusing when asked was considered rude and not allowed. However, I could sit down after one dance, which I did.

Between waitressing, schoolwork, and helping in the house, the next four years rushed by, interspersed with surgeries and deaths. The years 1951-1952 were stressful years health-wise for our family. Mother had a hysterectomy. She was hurt and angry when Father brought her home from the hospital, dumped her into bed, and then took off for the local tavern. All three of us had our tonsils removed. Susan's appendix burst after she jumped over a fence and ended up in the hospital having emergency surgery. The following year, my appendix was removed and Johnny was circumcised. He was in agony for weeks.

8. SCRIPTING

I came home from school one day to find Father sobbing in the middle of the dining room. His mother had died that morning. It was the only time I saw him cry. I didn't know how to comfort him and stood very still, in place, without saying a word. He could not stop crying for a long time. The next year, George, my favorite cousin died of Hodgkin's Lymphoma. He was only 28 years old. Aunt Rosi was heartbroken.

Life seemed so unfair. While other kids my age were out playing sports or taking piano lessons or ballet lessons, I was cooking, scrubbing floors, doing laundry, and waitressing. While their parents came to talk to their teachers and were interested in their children's schoolwork, no one ever came to see mine. Even when my essay won first prize from the Windsor Horticultural Society and my picture appeared in the Windsor newspaper, my parents were too busy with their own problems to even notice.

Mother was the one who paid the rent while Father spent his days drinking and smoking. She often told me the story of how they had met and fallen in love. Mother obviously married him for love. Curious, I once asked her, "How long did your *great love* last, Mom?"

Dead serious, without hesitating even for a moment, she replied, "About 30 days." Their marriage lasted until the day my father died.

"I'm never going to be at the mercy of any man to support me," I thought to myself. At the same time I concluded that if a man really loved his family, he would do anything to provide for them.

I graduated from Prince Edward as the top student and received the honor pin. As hard as I had worked for that pin, it did not bring me the satisfaction or joy I thought it would.

At W.D. Lowe Vocational School, I began preparing for a secretarial position along with all the others in my class. Here again, I did not have much in common with the other students. Most of my time was spent practicing typing and shorthand in addition to housework and waitressing.

I also won the public speaking contest and played varsity basketball in spite of being the shortest on the team. The first high school party I attended turned out to be a disaster. I purchased prizes with my own money, thinking there would be some sort of competitive games played at a high school party. However, my classmates were more interested in covering the host's bathroom ceiling with tomatoes. This was their idea of a good time? It was my first and last high school party.

Then, there was the embarrassing episode with my bomb fears. We were in the middle of an exam in tenth grade. As I glanced out the window, I noticed a plane followed by a sudden flash of light. It never occurred to me that this might be lightning since it was winter. The only thing I could think of was bombs.

Many years had passed since thoughts of bombs had entered my mind. War was a distant memory and not mentioned for a long time in our family. I thought my fears had disappeared for good. Now, they surfaced with a vengeance.

My reaction was immediate and automatic. Breathing became difficult, my skin became hot, and I began to sweat. Embarrassed, I reluctantly told the teacher what was happening to me. She allowed me to go to the bathroom to splash cold water on my face. It took a few minutes for my breathing to slow down.

After returning to class, the teacher kept her eyes on me. I wondered what she was thinking. Did she really believe me or did she suspect I was somehow trying to cheat on the exam? When the exam was over, I dragged myself home to face the never-ending family problems.

8. SCRIPTING

The job situation for my father never improved for very long. Consequently, my parents decided to leave Canada and move to the States. It was much easier to gain entry to the U.S. from Canada than it was from Austria. Their final destination, however, changed. My parents decided against moving to Columbus. Instead, they chose to move closer to relatives living in Royal Oak, Michigan. I also suspect that Mother wanted to stay as far away as possible from her brother George. Another important consideration was, by living in Royal Oak, Mother could keep her job in Detroit. Both counted on there being more job opportunities for my father in the Motor City.

Mother found an affordable apartment close to work in downtown Detroit. By taking up residency in the U.S., she began the immigration process for the family. On the weekends, she came home to Windsor with horror stories of the nightly arguments and fights in her apartment and her fears of going to sleep at night. As for crossing the Detroit-Windsor border, all she had to do was tell the custom agents that she was born in Youngstown, Ohio. She could move to the U.S. any time she wanted to, but Susan, Johnny, and Father needed to go through the U.S. Citizenship and Immigration Services. My status required that I move to the U.S. and claim my citizenship through naturalization before turning 21.

Finally, Uncle George left for Ohio to join his mother who had arrived in Columbus to be near her American son John and his girlfriend, Archie. Uncle George continued drinking and now made life miserable for his mother.

I expected things to improve. They did not. Even with Uncle George gone, the situation remained the same. Susan and I kept arguing. There was no steady job for my father. Mother never let Father forget how worthless he was and how disappointed she was in him. Father kept reiterating her disappointment. It became a vicious cycle of arguing. There was never enough money, and they still owed their souls to the Beneficial Finance Company.

In July 1955, one month before I turned 16, I met my future husband, Rudy. He and his parents arrived in Canada a few months earlier. We met at a German dance, and I gave him my phone number. A few days later, he called to ask me out. However, never having been on a date, I needed to get my mother's permission first. Not wanting him to know this, I told him I was busy that particular day. In the meantime, Mother gave her permission, and I could only hope that he would ask me again.

Rudy did call me again, and we started seeing each other regularly. Within a few months, we were discussing marriage.

Was 16 a particularly vulnerable age?
Was it hormones?
Was it a way of removing myself from all the turmoil and my dysfunctional family?
I don't really know, probably all of the above.
By the fall of that year, I decided to quit high school, get married, and move out of the house. I would never have to listen to another argument or take orders from anyone again.

School was mandatory until the age of 16 in Canada. I turned 16 a few days before the start of the fall term. This was probably the worst irreversible decision of my life. It also set a horrible example for Susan and Johnny. Eventually both dropped out of high school.

9. WORK – WEDDING – MARRIED LIFE

Instead of going back to school, I changed the birth date on my identification card from 1939 to 1937. Instantly, I became 18 years of age instead of 16 and had no difficulty getting a secretarial position at Michigan Mutual Liability Company in downtown Detroit. After a year, I quit and took a job as a statistical typist involved in copy and layout work for GM, which paid a heck of a lot more money.

Commuting through the Detroit-Windsor Tunnel, however, was a daily challenge because of my fear of closed spaces. As I watched people's faces on the bus, I wondered if anyone else suffered from the same problem. Trying to appear nonchalant while my breathing changed and my stomach tightened, I counted the seconds until the daylight appeared from the other side of the tunnel. It took a while for my breathing to become normal after exiting.

Regardless of how many times I crossed the border through that tunnel, my claustrophobia never improved, but this was the only way to make a halfway decent income. My parents did not charge me rent even though they could have used the money. Except for taxes and travel expenses, I stashed every cent I earned and then purchased my first car for $1,600 cash.

My car, job, and dating Rudy was proof to me I was now an adult even though I was only 17 years old. Rudy did not own a car, and we used mine to go to the movies and dances.

The first time I invited Rudy to a dance in the Saxon Hall, he ended up in a fistfight and blamed it on me. He complained a group of men had looked at him and laughed. Then he demanded to know *exactly* what I had done to make them laugh at him. I was so hurt and ashamed for myself and for my parents.

Since its founding, physical fights in the Saxon Hall were unheard of, which made it all the more embarrassing. This was supposed to be his introduction to the Saxon people. I wanted to be proud of him and make a good impression on my parents' friends. Even then, the sick feeling in my stomach told me this marriage was never going to work. Rudy was seven and a half years older than I was. Yet, his behavior came across as very immature.

I did not listen to my intuition and ignored all the warning signs. It seemed too late to change my mind. How could I undo everything I changed in my life because of him? Marriage seemed my only way out. In addition, I hoped God would understand as long as I obeyed Him and kept myself only to this one man.

My parents begged me not to quit school. After his fight in the Saxon Hall, Aunt Rosi and my cousins didn't like Rudy. They wanted me to stay in school. They were convinced I was too young for a serious relationship, and Rudy was not right for me. They wanted me to hold off on marriage.

His family felt the same. My relatives could not understand why he claimed to be German when his family spoke only Ukrainian in the house. To me this seemed silly. I didn't care what they spoke and wondered why anyone cared. Meanwhile, I spent as much time as possible teaching Rudy the English language.

We both ignored the red flags. Instead, we spent our time discussing plans to claim my U.S. citizenship, how to go about getting better jobs in the U.S., where to live, religion, and birth control. As it turned out, Rudy was in charge of birth control, and I was in charge of everything else.

9. WORK – WEDDING – MARRIED LIFE

Because the Catholic Church would not recognize our marriage, Rudy attended classes and was baptized Evangelical-Lutheran in our church. Apparently, he did not tell his parents until a week before our wedding. Upon hearing this news, his mother took off her shoe and smashed it across his face. The family considered themselves strict Catholics, although they followed only the rules they chose and everyone practiced birth control. They were not happy with him getting married, furious for changing his religion, and of course, I was to blame.

Their dislike of me seemed to be a class thing. His parents often spoke of the great life they had back in Romania. They were *city people,* living in a huge house with servants, custom-made clothing, and handmade shoes.

Rudy's parents were determined that Rudy should have a profession. He finished his dental education at the age of 23 before immigrating to Canada. However, Canada did not recognize his degree and required that he attend additional years of schooling in order to practice dentistry.

Not knowing the language and having already spent so many years in school, he had no choice but to accept a job working for an orthodontist as a dental technician for $75 a week. His friends laughed at him when they discovered they made more money than he did without higher education.

The GM production line did not require a college degree. It broke Rudy's spirit as well as his confidence. Nevertheless, we went ahead with our plans. Neither one of us was very enthusiastic about getting married.

A year later, I sold my car for $1,800 to pay for our wedding for 400 people. I also paid for Rudy's wedding suit and a $200 debt he had incurred by attending an orthodontic convention in Chicago.

The Saxon Hall could accommodate a maximum of 400 people according to the Windsor fire marshal. Of course, these were my parents' friends. My friends I could count on one hand. Those who did not get invitations were rather upset.

Although Aunt Rosi was against the marriage, she did everything she could to help with the plans. She rounded up about a dozen of her best friends who cooked and baked for a solid week. They prepared a feast of chicken, pork, cabbage rolls, salads, and an assortment of pastries for 400 people.

Each woman tried to outdo the other. Aunt Rosi only charged me for the cost of the food. They donated their labor along with most of the baked goods.

The rent for the hall was very reasonable since my parents were members. The biggest expense was the band and the alcohol for that many people. My wedding dress was custom-made by a local seamstress for all of $60 plus the material I provided. I was 17 years old.

It was customary to give only cash to the bride and groom. We ended up with $3,200, which to us was a small fortune in 1957. The wedding expenses added up to $1,700, which left us with $1,500 to begin our new life.

Unaware of it at the time, this would set the tone for our marriage. Like my mother before me, I was going to be the workhorse, and like my father, Rudy was not able to support me even though he was a college graduate. Responsibilities of any kind seemed to overwhelm him, and most of the time I made the decisions for both of us.

On my wedding day, I discovered that my father was laid off from his most recent job. My parents had gone to the Beneficial Finance Company yet again to borrow $500 for our wedding gift. Rudy's parents were much more sensible and gave us $50 without going into debt.

We spent one night in our $65 a month furnished apartment before leaving for Niagara Falls on our honeymoon. Each passing day got worse. Neither one of us was happy. All I could do was worry about my parents going into debt because

9. WORK – WEDDING – MARRIED LIFE

of me, while Rudy worried about his mother being angry that he had married *me*. We came home a week early from our honeymoon to figure out what to do next.

I canceled our lease on the apartment, and my new husband and I moved in with my parents. We paid them $80 per month for the next seven months so they could repay the loan to the Beneficial Finance Company.

Rudy's parents were furious. Then we moved in with them while we applied for our U.S. residency in order to claim my U.S. citizenship and to find a better-paying job for Rudy.

His parents hated that we were moving to the U.S. because of me. They could not acknowledge the fact that there was no way Rudy could make a decent living and support a wife in Windsor. There were many more opportunities for him in the States. I didn't have a choice. If I wanted to claim my U.S. citizenship, I needed to live in the States by the age of 21. On his own, the waiting period for Rudy to get into the U.S. was nine years.

At the time, the American government was drafting young men into the army. His parents and relatives worried that Rudy might be drafted. They left Germany because they did not want their son to serve in the German Army. Now, there was a slight chance that he could be drafted by living in the United States.

Rudy also told me he had gotten a girl pregnant in Germany. He only shared this bit of information with me for fear that one of his friends would tell me. However, his parents instead of having him take responsibility for his actions, supported him in running away from both.

Meanwhile, Rudy needed a job in Michigan. Therefore, I began making lists of orthodontists in the Detroit area out of the phone book. Narrowing it down to 15 orthodontists—as uncomfortable as it was for me to do—I began calling them until Rudy received a job offer.

10. COMING TO AMERICA

We bought our first house, a three-bedroom, one-bath, 1,000 square foot home in Lincoln Park, Michigan, only a few miles from where Rudy worked. In 1960, we moved into our new home, neither one of us very happy in our marriage. Every morning I took the bus to work from Lincoln Park to Detroit and then walked home after work from the bus stop.

Most of our neighbors were young couples raising families. A few months after we moved in, I began feeling sick. My new friend Rosemary across the street gave me the name of her old country doctor, Dr. Clark.

There are no words for the shock I felt on the examining table when this doctor told me that I was pregnant. "Are you sure?" I asked in disbelief.

"Of course," Dr. Clark replied smiling. "You are about five or six weeks pregnant."

My mind went blank after that, and I couldn't get out of his office fast enough. Somehow, I managed the long walk home in a daze. How could I be pregnant? Rudy was in charge of birth control. His method worked for us for more than five years. Now, suddenly it stopped working? Had he deliberately gotten me pregnant?

Our agreement not to have children went back to when we first met in 1955. For me, my decision not to bring children into this world went back much further to the age of seven in the Austrian cottage.

That evening, when I told him I was pregnant, there was absolutely no response, no surprise. He had nothing to say.

10. COMING TO AMERICA

We never discussed having children because he knew how I felt from the very beginning. However, my pregnancy was the added insurance policy he needed to keep himself from being drafted.

His deliberate selfish betrayal left a bitter taste in my mouth. I immediately gave my two-week notice at work. Rudy was not happy at being the sole breadwinner and often came home miserable from work. My misery revolved around being terrified of childbirth, recalling my mother's horror stories of her experiences throughout my formative years.

Regardless of how many times I begged my mother for the secret formula to end my pregnancy, she refused to give it to me. Mother had often discussed this brew with me. A young nurse in Youngstown, Ohio, had given this recipe to my Grandmother Gramelt. She, in turn, handed it down to her daughter Mary, and now I wanted it for myself, but Mother's unwavering "no" prevailed.

Later I learned this concoction consisted of carbolic acid, also known as phenol, Fels-Naptha soap, and camphor. Legal abortions after *Roe v Wade* would not exist in the United States until 1973.

Rudy and I did not talk much for the next six months. I spent most of that time crying. Every Sunday, I watched him get into the car for his weekly visit with his family. They could all rest easy now—no draft for Rudy. They could all celebrate! Feeling betrayed by Rudy and left again to fend for myself by my mother, I pondered if committing suicide was more painful than childbirth.

Kurt was born in February of 1961 and Ernst in November of 1962. My third pregnancy in 1963 ended in a *miscarriage*. I lost all confidence in my husband being in charge of birth control and took matters into my own hands. Now, I was in charge of everything while listening to Rudy complain daily how miserable he was at work, yet not doing anything to remedy the situation.

It was obvious to anyone who spent five minutes with him how much he hated to go to work. He was working for three orthodontists who barely paid him a living wage. Our house cost $15,900. At the time, we could not qualify for a mortgage on his salary. I encouraged him to go into business for himself. However, he lacked the confidence to even consider this.

It took two years until he finally agreed to invest all of $500 to build the necessary workbenches along with the required equipment. We found an inexpensive space on the main street in Lincoln Park, and I began calling orthodontists asking if any needed help with their orthodontic appliances.

Patients wear these appliances for a time to stabilize their teeth after orthodontic treatment. Other orthodontic devices are for simple cases when full-mouth banding is not required or where the arch needs a minimum amount of expanding.

Plasterwork, such as pouring impressions of teeth, is considered the lowliest of dental work and requires the least amount of expertise, schooling, and training. Rudy did not want to do plasterwork. Plasterwork was simply beneath him.

Because I wanted to help, I began training myself processing these plaster casts. Rudy took impressions of my teeth along with Kurt's teeth. Then I practiced pouring and trimming these casts, appropriately called "study models" repeatedly for days and weeks in our basement. If one was not up to my standards, I re-poured the impressions, regardless of how long it took to perfect each set of models.

By law, orthodontists are required to keep "before treatment" and "after treatment" plaster casts of their patients' teeth as permanent records. This made my end of the business repeat business, whereas the appliances Rudy created were not required for every patient at the end of their treatment.

10. COMING TO AMERICA

We both were happy when Rudy brought home the first impressions an orthodontist sent to him. I must have processed that set of models at least five times. It took days. I wanted the models to be beyond perfect. Apparently, the doctor liked my work, and eventually he sent all his dental impressions to me.

After I poured these impressions into molds, they hardened overnight. The following day, I ground them on a machine to standardized measurements, then sculpted, stamped, soaped, and polished them, all for the grand price of $4.50 per set. At first, each set of study models took hours to finish. With time and a lot of practice, I became more proficient until I could process a set (upper and lower), in one hour.

Approximately a year and a half later, I raised the price to $5 per set, and I immediately lost one orthodontist. Persistent, I kept on sending out brochures and continued adding accounts to Rudy's Orthodontic Laboratory. Slowly, the business began to grow. Working out of my home made it possible to earn money, and at the same time, raise our two boys myself.

Neither my husband nor I knew how to parent. The last thing I wanted to do was use my parents as role models. If anything, I wanted to do the exact opposite of what they had done. There were no classes we could take. Like most new parents, we learned on the job.

I noticed the high school dropout rate was much higher in our blue-collar area than in the northern suburbs of Detroit. I felt our boys would have a better chance at a decent education in the more affluent northern suburbs. There, most of the parents were college graduates, and the children were expected to follow their example. Also, most of the orthodontists who sent work to Rudy had their offices in these suburbs.

It made sense to me to move to West Bloomfield where a new subdivision was being built. One Sunday, Rudy and I drove to look at these new model homes. A five-bedroom, tri-level was within our price range. The only thing it did not have was a basement, which of course I wanted. However, it did have a very large walled-off storage space in front of the two-plus car garage, and we decided to purchase this model. All my husband talked about was how difficult the move would be. He felt overwhelmed as usual, and as usual, I ended up taking care of everything.

We were able to save the real estate commission on the sale of our Lincoln Park house because I sold the house myself. When Rudy joined his friends on a ski trip, I moved the family to our new home in West Bloomfield, furnished most of it, and set up my workshop in the fifth bedroom downstairs next to the family room. This workroom, approximately 13 by 13 feet, would be my life for many years while raising our boys. This lowly plasterwork enabled us to give them a life that I could never have imagined for myself when I was growing up.

11. RAISING TWO BOYS AS AMERICANS

After we enrolled the boys in school in West Bloomfield, their teachers told me both Kurt and Ernst were behind in a couple subjects. However, they assured me that neither would have a problem catching up. My intuition had been right. The school system was better in this area. I was certain the move was the right decision. Not only was I hoping for a better education for the boys, but I also wanted better allergy and asthma doctors for Ernst.

Next, we had to find office space for my husband's business. The daily commute back to Lincoln Park was simply too far and took too long. I began searching for commercial office space. In our new area, office space was astronomically expensive.

One day, while scouting for rental space, I met this wonderful architect named Jim. He had approximately 800 square feet unfinished space available next to his office on the most expensive business street in the area. We sat and talked for several hours on his deck outside his office.

The space he had was perfect! So was the rent of $150 per month. This was a fraction of all the other estimates on my list. Jim finished the workroom beautifully, complete with a bathroom. Above the two workbenches I planned on having built, he installed boxed-in fluorescent lighting in stained wood.

Jim made it possible for us to raise our children in West Bloomfield. All those years, up to the time Rudy died, Jim never raised the rent. I am eternally grateful to this kind and generous man.

That same handyman I met in a hardware store in Lincoln Park built the workbenches for the new lab. He also completed my workroom in our home in West Bloomfield. Then he built a 4 foot by 4 foot walnut-colored Formica cube on casters with a huge drawer for all the children's toys for the family room. It matched the Magnavox TV-record player combination perfectly. When the boys were through playing with their toys, they deposited them inside this beautiful cube.

Rudy went on another ski trip, and I moved all the workbenches into his new office space. Then I sent out flyers to his accounts announcing the new location of Rudy's Orthodontic Laboratory.

The years rushed by. My part of the business grew while Rudy's did not. I stopped sending out flyers for my husband's business. Rudy would not pick up the phone or drop in on any of the orthodontists who were potential new accounts. His business did not grow. My end of the business would not stop growing, and I was buried in plaster in my cubicle for many years.

One of the neighbors asked Ernst, "What does your mother do all day in the house?" "She works" he replied.

It must have seemed rather normal to both my children. It was all the boys had ever known. I made it look easy. Whenever one of them needed me, I immediately stopped working and tended to their needs. Neither of the boys was aware of the toll it was taking on me. They grew up with me working, but always nearby and available to them when they needed me. It never occurred to me that someone else should provide childcare for me.

After more than ten years, my price per set of study models gradually increased to $15, but each set still took an hour to complete, regardless of how fast I worked. It ended

11. RAISING TWO BOYS AS AMERICANS

up with me working seven days a week, 80 to 90 hours per week. My callused hands looked like I was a bricklayer, while Rudy worked 30 hours and spent his weekends visiting his relatives.

Both boys loved West Bloomfield, grew, and flourished in that suburb. Meanwhile, I desperately hoped the little white gloves Doris Day wore in the movies would come back in vogue. That way I could hide my callused hands.

I longed to get a break from all the work and the monotony of my life. Again, I wanted more. This Déjà Vu feeling went all the way back to my childhood. Now, I wanted Rudy to be more of a husband and father and to pitch in with the responsibilities involved in both. I wanted to get rid of my calluses, have him promote his business, and take some of the load off me. But as far as I could tell, marketing his skills to grow the business in order to be able to hire a technician was never even a consideration.

The extra workbench I had built for his laboratory was obviously my dream for the business and not his. Not once did he pick up that phone and call an orthodontist. Instead, he constantly escaped to Windsor to visit his parents and relatives. There, he spent his time listening to the same WWI stories from his father he had heard since he was a child.

His uncle and aunt badmouthed me constantly. I was never good enough for him. They never acknowledged how hard I worked. It seemed the more I worked, the happier Rudy became since it kept me in the house barely having time to go out for groceries. He even hated when I left the house to finish my high school education in a nearby town. Instead of supporting me, it was a constant battle regardless of what I did if it meant me leaving the house. Even reading a book *in the house,* intimidated him.

Once I got so absorbed in reading *Atlas Shrugged* by Ayn Rand, I spent the whole night reading. When Rudy came down the following morning and found me on the sofa in the living room still reading, he was quite upset. His last words to me before leaving for work and slamming the door to the garage were, "If I read as many books as you read, I would be a professor by now." During our 20-plus years of marriage, I never once saw my husband pick up a book, not in German and not in English.

Returning home from one of his Sunday visits to his aunt and uncle, Rudy was particularly upset. His aunt had exclaimed to everyone in his presence, "Look what she has done to him. He was such a beautiful doll!" Rudy appeared crushed.

Exactly what had I done to him, except work my butt off? This ignorant woman didn't realize she was hurting Rudy with her remarks, not me.

His aunt's remarks upset him so much that he ran to the nearest mirror to examine himself. Then he retreated to our bedroom and stayed there until the following morning.

Not once did my husband pitch in with our house, take care of the boys, attend a PTA meeting, or pace the hospital corridor when Ernst was having an asthma attack. It all fell on me. All the while, his family never accepted me. Rather, they put me down at every opportunity.

Even his sister visiting from Germany had to take a swipe at me while accepting my hospitality. Rudy never once defended or stood up for me. He simply could not cut that mother-son bond with his family. The boys and I never came first in his life. Consequently, there was no intimate bond between us. I was never considered "his family." Kurt and Ernst only became important to him after I filed for divorce. He used them as a means of punishing me for leaving him.

11. RAISING TWO BOYS AS AMERICANS

Visions of both my sons attending college somewhere and me getting a divorce began occupying my mind more frequently. After the boys finished high school, I did not care what happened. The sole responsibility of raising the boys, especially Ernst, along with working round the clock, had taken its toll. To make matters worse, my doctor told me I needed surgery. How was I going to manage that?

12. FIRING GOD

I had no illusions about Rudy being capable of giving me the emotional support I needed so desperately. My parents were left totally in the dark regarding my surgery. Going it alone had become a way of life for me. In spite of my fears, I began preparing for major surgery, certain I would die.

All the insurance policies were updated, and the house sparkled from top to bottom. Everyone's laundry was completed, folded, and back in their drawers. There were enough cooked meals wrapped and frozen for at least a month. The 700 pound freezer was filled to the brim. This would give Rudy time to get his bearings while getting used to taking care of the house and the boys by himself. Kurt was 16 and Ernst 15. Kurt had just gotten his first driver's license. Both boys were at a stage where they could pretty much take care of themselves.

My older son dropped me off at the hospital. Alone, I signed myself in. I remember lying on the gurney in front of the surgery room as my doctor approached. When I told him how certain I was that I was going to die, he offered no comfort or conversation. He simply shook his head and walked away.

A wonderful black nurse walked over to me and held my hand. She overheard my conversation with the surgeon and tried to reassure me things would be okay as two other gowned assistants began wheeling me into the operating room. The room spun as the shot they gave me began taking effect. My eyes closed and I began descending into the deep.

12. FIRING GOD

When I awoke, I was alone in the room. It took some time to realize I had not died. I was still alive.

Even this, God had screwed up.

I was supposed to die, yet here I was, still alive. A lifetime of disappointments rushed over me. All the praying I did throughout my life—all the praying my mother and grandmother did—not once did God help us. Frustration, anger, and disappointment overwhelmed me. Tears filled my eyes.

"I have had it with you, God!" I said aloud, my eyes on the ceiling. "I followed all your rules—never stole, never lied, never cheated. I did everything by the book, *your book, your rules*. I obeyed every commandment and dogma you ever gave me. I'm sick of being meek and humble. Do you hear me, God? Are you listening, God? This is the end of the line. This is all I can take."

By this time, I was close to screaming. "Exactly what plan would it spoil if I were just a little bit happy? And that reward you are always promising—you know what you can do with that reward, God? You can stick it in your ear, God. You're fired!"

With tears streaming down my face, my nose running, I gasped for air while holding my aching stomach. "YOU ARE FIRED, FIRED, FIRED!" I screamed at the top of my lungs. "DO YOU HEAR ME, GOD? From now on, I am going to be in charge of my life. No more asking you for anything—nothing—ever again."

Hearing my screams, two nurses came running into the room. That day, I fired God, fired my husband, fired my in-laws, fired my husband's miserable aunt and uncle, and fired everyone who disrespected me.

Nothing mattered anymore, not even if God struck me dead right then and there. In fact, I expected it. I was ready for it.

A few days later, my son came to drive me home. My heart ached as we passed my husband's lab. He would not take the time to drive me home himself even though he only worked about 30 hours a week to my 90.

When Rudy came home that day, he began experiencing stomach problems. I had surgery—he was having stomach pain. So, as usual, he drove to Windsor to his "family" to be babied by his father, stepmother, aunt, and uncle. He was incapable of making a bowl of soup for me or comforting me in any way. Meanwhile, I really did expect to be struck by lightning by this angry, vengeful God.

There was no help before I went into the hospital and no help after I came home from the hospital. Rudy was too busy taking care of himself. In order to get a glass of milk or make myself a cup of coffee, I scooched down one step at a time on my butt from the upper part of our tri-level to get to the kitchen. Slowly, I recovered. My husband's stomach problems got worse.

I felt hurt. This man was incapable of empathy, sympathy, or compassion for me while I was trying to recuperate. At the time, I was not astute enough to realize how terrified he was of having the responsibility of taking care of the house and the children on his own. This narcissist, this mama's boy, was terrified that he would not be able to manage without me. Had he been honest and shared his fears with me, it would probably have saved our marriage. Instead, he lashed out at me and told me that five weeks was plenty of time to recuperate. Rudy wanted me back at work regardless of how I felt.

13. A GIFT OF GRACE

The woman who entered that hospital really did die. Although it was not a physical death, nevertheless, it was a death. From that day on, I knew that regardless of what else happened in my life I was worthy—worthy of respect, worthy of love, worthy of being treated with kindness. If my husband were incapable of giving these to me, I would give them to myself.

When I read William Blake's poem, "A Little Boy Lost," it touched me at a very deep level, especially these two lines:

'Nought loves another as itself,
Nor venerates another so,

These lines stayed with me, and I began looking at myself with as much objectivity as possible. It became obvious to me that throughout our marriage, I had never loved myself or put myself first but rather last at every turn. My life amounted to pleasing everyone *except* myself. Everyone was more important than I was.

I wondered if this was my way of avoiding arguing.

I allowed this kind of behavior toward me, regardless of my rationalizations. I alone had the power to change it. No more being a doormat for anyone. No more being the butt of cruel jokes. No more aching as my partner in life conspired openly to destroy my spirit and my humanity. Regardless of how many times he and his relatives tried crushing me, my spirit kept rising and screaming to be set free. For more than 20 years, I listened to my husband's condescending and abusive language toward me. No more!

Rudy's last humiliation came after my six-week checkup, post-surgery. It was the final straw. Having a hysterectomy seemed to affect him more than it did me. As for me, there was only gratitude. There would be no more betrayal of my trust, no more surprise pregnancies to keep me chained.

My intent as far back as I can remember was to get a divorce after Kurt and Ernst finished high school. This was the only thing that made the abuse tolerable. Now, two more years of abuse until Ernst finished high school was unacceptable. Did I even have two more years? Could I tolerate his abuse for another two years? The answer was a resounding NO!

I sat my husband down and poured out my grievances then gave him six months to file for divorce. He could tell all his relatives who had never accepted me that he was finally getting rid of this stupid, ugly bitch—his favorite names for me. My last words to him were, "If you don't file for divorce, Rudy, by the end of six months, I *will* file." I could only imagine how happy his whole family would be.

Counting down the months as each passed, I kept reminding him. At the end of six months, he had no intention of filing for divorce but simply ignored me, nor did he stop putting me down, calling me names, or agree to seek professional help as a couple. He liked things as they were. I, on the other hand, had put up with 20 plus years of abuse so the boys could be raised with both a mother and a father in West Bloomfield. He did not listen to anything I said or take me seriously. The six months were up in November, and I filed for divorce. As soon as I filed, I called my parents.

All those years I was married, not once had I complained to my parents. They had no idea how unhappy I felt. I made my choice at age 16. What purpose would it serve to share

13. A GIFT OF GRACE

my misery with them? Now, here I was informing them I was getting a divorce. No surprise to me, in a casual dismissive voice, my mother's response was, "You're not getting a divorce, Marie."

I looked straight into her eyes and repeated, "Mom, I'm getting a divorce, and I wanted to tell you myself instead of you hearing it from the relatives."

This time with more certainty in her voice she again said, "I know you, Marie. You're not getting a divorce."

"Okay, Mom, believe whatever you want" I replied, exasperated.

Like Rudy, she too invalidated anything I said. Like Rudy, she didn't really know me at all. *But then, how could she?* I asked myself. For more than 20 years, I never shared with her how miserable married life really was for me. Both mistook my quietness and distaste for arguing for weakness.

Not one of Rudy's relatives, my in-laws or his aunt and uncle ever spoke to me again. They were angrier with me now than before I filed for divorce. All of them worked diligently at turning my sons against me. It was the *only* way they could hurt me. I never grieved even for a moment over this abusive marriage. Twenty-plus years of grieving was more than enough, and now it was finally going to end. I could not have been happier—willing to be struck by lightning if that was going to be my finale.

As the weeks passed, instead of being struck by lightning, this incredible peace came over me. It was the kind of peace I only heard about in church, a peace that passes all understanding, a peace that can only be called *grace*. With it came the understanding that grace was not given to me because I earned or deserved it for being good. *Grace was an unmerited, undeserved, merciful gift to me when I least expected it.* This grace only grew within me from that day on.

At the time, however, my logical mind could not understand how, in the midst of all the family chaos, I was deliriously happy. Nothing bothered me. It was sheer bliss! My beautiful children, who were never disrespectful or cruel, suddenly become tyrants and imitated their abusive father's cruelty. Ernst appeared to believe the worse he treated me, the more his father would love him.

It never occurred to me that the bond I had with them since birth could ever be tarnished, much less broken. I was the one who was there for them 24/7. Their father was never there for any of their needs. Now, it seemed as though that bond had never even existed. Their father instilled in them that I was the villain who destroyed the family since I was the one who was getting the divorce.

Rudy stayed in the master bedroom during the divorce while I moved into the spare bedroom. He dragged the divorce out by putting the sale price of the home much too high. There were no buyers even interested in looking at the place, much less making an offer. Later that year my husband told me that he thought I was going through midlife crisis. If he dragged it out long enough, I would change my mind about the divorce. He was sadly mistaken.

All those years, telling him I was going to leave him had fallen on deaf ears and had been ignored. All the times when I refused to engage him in arguments but rather kept repeating, "Rudy, I am going to divorce you if you don't stop calling me names and putting me down. Start taking some responsibility for raising the boys."

Laughing, he often said, "Well, you take the first 20 years, and I'll take the next 20."

It never occurred to him even for a moment that I meant every word. He dismissed me and his verbal abuse continued. After so many years, I doubt he was even aware of how much pain he'd inflicted. How could I have any

13. A GIFT OF GRACE

feelings for a man who treated me with such cruelty and contempt?

Rudy was so mean-spirited he reported me to the city for running a business out of my home. He was actually trying to keep me from earning a living. His vindictiveness for leaving him knew no bounds.

One morning, the West Bloomfield City Manager contacted me and informed me that my husband had reported me for running a business out of my home. He continued, "When your son reported you, I simply threw the report in the trash. However, now that your husband has filed a formal complaint against you, I have to follow up. What exactly are you doing in your house that is so dangerous?"

I laughed and told him, "I'm in the process of getting a divorce and am not turning my paycheck over to him anymore."

Understanding, he replied, "This complaint is going on the bottom of a very full complaint drawer." I thanked him and hung up.

Finally, the court date arrived. My husband sat on one side with his attorney. I sat on the other side with my attorney. The judge was sitting behind his desk which was positioned at the front of the room centered between the two sides.

The whole process took less than an hour. Near the end, I reminded my attorney that I wanted my name back. My attorney addressed the judge, requesting the restoration of my maiden name. The judge in turn asked my husband's attorney, who then turned to Rudy and asked him if that was acceptable to him.

Unbelievable! Here I had just divorced this man, yet he controlled whether or not I would get my name back. To me, this was the height of absurdity. This judge gave my ex-husband the power to decide whether I could have my maiden name restored. What would my options have been had he not agreed? Dismissing the thought, I focused on being grateful that it was finally over.

Rudy stood up and lunged toward me. The judge jumped out of his chair, believing that my now ex-husband was going to attack me. Instead, he grabbed me, hugged me, and congratulated me on the divorce. Rudy then turned toward the judge, saluted him, and marched out of the courtroom like a soldier. The whole scene was surreal.

I arrived home ahead of him. It was finally over. I crawled into my bed in the spare bedroom feeling numb. A few minutes later Rudy walked in, sat at the foot of the bed, and began sobbing. Obviously, he had left his macho act in the courtroom. Feeling sorry for him, I got up and held him in my arms.

Suddenly, the bedroom door flung open and Ernst walked in. He took one look at us, turned on his heels, and walked out slamming the door behind him.

It took me a long time to figure out what had just happened. The only thing I could come up with was he had a father for the first time in his life and was not about to lose him, not even to his mother. My heart went out to him, reflecting on all the cruelty the two had inflicted on me as a team. Now, here we were, seemingly embracing.

It must have felt like total betrayal to my son. My very soul ached for him. There was no way to comfort him. He had made his choice.

Rudy and I were officially divorced, but the house was still up for sale with no buyers in sight. Rudy still lived in the house and I tried to stay away as much as possible.

At the time, my attorney warned me, "If you do not buy him out, someone like me will pick up your house for a song, and you will both lose."

In order to save myself, I would have to save my now ex-husband. My end of the business, the means by which I

13. A GIFT OF GRACE

supported myself, was in my workroom downstairs. What choice did I have?

My grandmother loaned me the money to buy my husband's share in the house. Rudy and Ernst finally moved out. Of course, at the time, I did not know that Rudy hadn't paid the property taxes on the house for several years. After I filed for divorce, I stopped taking care of the bills for the house. Rudy simply disregarded the tax notices. He cheated me out of several thousand dollars. It didn't matter. Nothing mattered. I was finally in a position to concentrate on myself for the first time in my life.

The divorce, sale of the house, and settling the finances took the better part of three years. The cruelty I endured from Rudy and my younger son was enough to last me several lifetimes. Never again would I place myself at the mercy of any man. Having fired God and taken responsibility for it by being willing to accept anything that happened to me gave me enormous confidence.

How could I ever allow another man to abuse me?
Never again, I swore to myself.

Only my children kept me from divorcing Rudy during the first few years after they were born. Staying in the marriage may have been a horrible decision. At the time, however, the alternative seemed much worse, especially after observing the misery of several of my children's friends who had two and three sets of parents. I was determined to endure anything not to consign my sons to that fate.

Ernst, the great manipulator, told me, "If I go with you, Mom, Dad is going to be really mad. But if I go with Dad, I know you'll understand."

I agreed, if that is what he wanted, but not before discussing it with two therapists. Both told me that males usually identify with their father. Ernst needed his father, who because of Ernst's many health issues had been absent from his life since birth. By contrast, Ernst and I were joined at the hip since his birth *because* of his many health issues. Rudy resented Ernst for getting all my attention. At the age of 15, the last thing I wanted to do was keep him from his father. I used to hide him when he had an asthma attack so his father wouldn't yell at him. Rudy always blamed Ernst for his asthma attacks and insisted on knowing where he had been to induce the attack. Now his father, not wanting to pay child support, suddenly became his best friend. Ernst loved it!

Kurt told me that he wanted to stay with me, which made me very happy. He was away at college for most of the time after I filed for divorce. He did not participate in the ugly, cruel behavior of his younger brother and his father.

Nevertheless, if Kurt wanted to live in my house, he would have to follow my house rules. After almost three years of daily disrespect and abuse, I would no longer tolerate any of it, not from anyone.

As soon as I told him, he was furious. Having been raised with a sense of entitlement, he did not intend to follow anyone's rules except his own. He decided against living with me and moved in with his father instead, but not before taking his fist and smashing a hole in the drywall. I ignored it, helped him pack, wished him well, and hired someone to fix the wall.

Kurt decided to drop out of college to pursue bodybuilding, insisting that it would only be for one semester. I pleaded with him not to do this, never disclosing how disappointed I was, and refrained from putting a guilt trip on him.

However, my grand plans for him ended abruptly after he announced his decision. The whole reason for moving to West Bloomfield was to give him and his brother a better education and more opportunities. It was not for their father who disliked the area and never felt comfortable

13. A GIFT OF GRACE

living there. And it certainly wasn't for me. My life consisted of getting more and more calluses sculpting dental casts. Growing up, both boys had been given the freedom to do pretty much anything they wanted as long as they took responsibility for it. How was Kurt going to take responsibility for dropping out of school? Bodybuilding was not going to pay his rent.

After he totaled the second car I paid for, I finally had enough. I added up the price of those two cars then divided the amount by ten, the average price of one set of study models over the years. Each set of casts took one hour to complete, regardless of how proficient I became at processing them. Then, I figured out how many hundreds of hours I spent in my cubicle in order to purchase these two cars for him.

Now he needed a third car. The straw that broke the camel's back was when he casually said to me, "Well, you know, Mom. I don't want to drive a tin can."

For a moment, I sat silently, taking that in. Then, looking at him calmly, I replied, "God forbid you should drive a tin can, Kurt. You can drive any car you want, any car your heart desires—because this time you are paying for it yourself."

That did not go over very well, but I was dead serious. The time had come for him to grow up. I taught him how to walk and now it was time to teach him how to walk away. Tough love is just that—tough.

During this post-surgery period, I took time for self-reflection. Evaluating everything I considered the "garbage" of my life, I saw how that garbage shaped and created the person I had become.

In spite of the constant verbal abuse, humiliations, and two occasions of physical abuse, *I liked myself*, knew I deserved better, and did not fear supporting myself or being on my own. The only thing I wanted out of this divorce was my name back, which thankfully the judge restored.

Thinking back on my life, I tried to be as objective as possible. Why did I marry this man? Was my life better with him? Did he take an interest in the children and their activities? How did he support me emotionally and financially? How did he and his whole family treat me? How did his relatives make me feel? And, most important of all, did I ever feel loved by this man?

In every category, he came up wanting. Plain common sense told me I was far better off without him. Saving my soul was worth any price required of me.

My ex-husband was furious most days and accused me of manipulating everything. In essence, I simply accepted anything that happened without caring about the outcome. *Undauntable, i*s the only word that comes to mind. I was happy when things went well for me and happy when things did not go well. ...

It always came down to the same understanding, which I began to apply to everyone in my life. "Father, forgive them for they know not what they do." Understanding and forgiving, however, did not mean I should continue to stay in a bad situation.

After all the abuse from Rudy, I felt no animosity toward my ex-husband. If anything, I felt sorry for him because he really did not know any better. My anger towards everyone who mistreated me disappeared. My only explanation of how this happened is by a complete change in attitude directly attributable to the gift of grace. This seemed the only plausible answer.

My father especially became a huge symbol of my change in attitude. Having been angry with him for most of my life for not financially supporting our family, I "saw" how his very actions made me more self-sufficient. I reevaluated each negative incident in my life and "saw" the good in it. All my garbage gradually became the gems of my life.

13. A GIFT OF GRACE

Then, for the first time I left my workroom and began exploring places outside my 13 x 13 cubicle in my home. Constantly trying to lose weight, I decided to check out Overeaters Anonymous. When I called them, they gave me their schedule, and I planned on attending their next meeting. As it turned out, their weekly meetings were held in a church only a few miles from my house.

14. A RADICAL CHANGE IN ATTITUDE

At my first Overeaters Anonymous (OA) meeting, someone handed me a copy of the twelve steps of Alcoholics Anonymous (AA). As I read them, I was amazed to find I'd accomplished most of the steps without having known about them. For me the best part of attending OA was simply meeting like-minded people who accepted me. They welcomed me and offered me their friendship while sharing their personal struggles.

After one of the meetings, a woman invited me to join her for a guided meditation at Cranbrook House in Bloomfield Hills. The Institute for Advanced Pastoral Studies (IAPS) was housed on the third floor. They were offering a guided meditation to anyone interested. Sure, I answered, not knowing what "meditation" meant. IAPS, I discovered, was only ten minutes from where I lived.

Hurriedly, we entered a huge dimly lit room on the first floor of the building. There must have been somewhere between 50 and 75 people seated in a circle. We barely had time to sit down in the two remaining chairs before the instructor began.

"Close your eyes," he said. "Inhale slowly and hold it, now exhale slowly, breathe, and relax into the chair." After repeating this several times, he continued, "Now, place your attention in the space between your foot and your ankle."

So that's what I did. Ever so slowly, he worked his way up to the knees, the hips, the stomach, solar plexus, the heart, and the throat. The instructor's voice was mesmerizing,

14. A RADICAL CHANGE IN ATTITUDE

hypnotic. Suddenly, something shifted in my mind. I was in another place, cold and dark. I had no body, yet I "saw" myself moving forward, almost as if in a darkened church. It became eerily quiet. There were no thoughts. Even the instructor's voice stopped.

Fear set in, and I jerked back into the room and my chair. Trembling and frozen in place with my eyes wide open, I waited for the meditation to end. The instructor then asked the audience to share their experiences.

People began sharing wonderful stories. Then the instructor asked, "Did anyone have a negative experience?"

Quickly, I scanned the circle of people expecting hands to go up. Nobody raised a hand. Was I the only person who had a negative experience? No way was I going to share my horrible experience with all these strangers. I leaned over to the woman who had invited me and told her that I did not feel well and had to leave. She led me into the kitchen and handed me a glass of water.

Apparently, someone ran to get the instructor to help me. The instructor hurried in and stood before me. I found out later his name was Jack. Looking down at me, he asked me what my experience had been. With my whole body visibly trembling, I described as best I could how, during the meditation, I entered some other place—a dark, cold, scary place. "Nothing like that has ever happened to me" I hastened to add.

He listened attentively and then asked me what my religious background was. I stared up at him. When I saw his face, it felt as though I had known this man for a thousand years. "Lutheran" I answered, trying desperately to stop shaking, not able to take my eyes off him.

Then, in an ever so gentle voice, he asked, "Would you like to pray?" Stunned, I backed away from him not wanting to believe what I heard.

Praying was the help he was going to give me? Oh – my – God! My mind was racing. "Praying" was his answer? Are you kidding me! That's all you've got? Really? Are you out of your mind? Here I'm scared to death and you want me to pray? Pray to this miserable God I fired a few months ago — this God?

Struggling to sound composed and trying not to show my utter disappointment, I said, "No thank you," as calmly as I could muster. "I'm going home."

As a result of following his instructions, his so-called "guided meditation" somehow I was transported to a horrible place. Yet he knew nothing about helping me understand what happened to me. God certainly wasn't going to help me. Even here, I was on my own again.

At home, I threw off my clothes, jumped into bed, got into the fetal position, pulled the covers over my head, and kept on shivering. I could not get that awful place out of my mind.

Where was this place? What was this place?

Who could I possibly ask and why did I enter this horrible place? Why was I the only person who had a negative experience? It would be many weeks before I summoned up enough courage to return to the Institute. My negative experience was never mentioned again during the three years I spent there, while the memory of it was always with me.

As the months passed, I became more and more comfortable at this extraordinary organization. The Institute became my refuge, as a completely new world opened up to me. Here, I found wonderful people who supported, accepted, and appreciated me. Besides doing clerical work, I attended every lecture and workshop offered at IAPS, as well as many other seminars.

14. A RADICAL CHANGE IN ATTITUDE

One of the "other" workshops was the *est Training*. This Training was offered over a two-weekend (60-hour) course known officially as The est Standard Training. Approximately 200 men and women participated in each workshop. We were all required to sign contracts to the effect that if anyone disrupted the workshop, they could be physically removed at the trainer's discretion.

This training claimed that it brought to the forefront the ideas of transformation, personal responsibility, accountability, and possibility. I took this course twice—once following all the rules—no watches, food, or bathroom breaks, etc. The second time, I broke all the rules to see if it made any difference in the outcome. It did not.

Why did this est Training not have an effect on me?

Not even at the very end of the training when former graduates joined the present graduates could I connect with the exuberant celebratory excitement of all these people. Curiously, I left with more questions than answers. Is this how groups are brainwashed?

When I returned to IAPS, I asked Jack if he had been caught up in this closing part of the training. "Oh yes," he replied, "very much so." That surprised me. Jack described his experience in detail after he took the est Training.

During the training, he vehemently disagreed with the trainers on many of their teachings. With his Doctor of Theology degree, years of counseling clergy from around the country, and vast knowledge of churches and religions, he was a formidable dissenter in this group. The est trainers for some reason decided to allow his continued loud disruptions. By the second weekend, he lost his voice from shouting so much. Yet, despite his many disagreements, he was swept up into the group excitement at the end. I paid twice for this training without it having any effect on me. "Why?" I wondered.

Nevertheless, the est Training continued to be popular, and for some it was life-altering. Est was considered part of the Human Potential Movement (HPM). While I didn't get anything out of est, the HPM, which began in the 1960s, definitely did have an effect on me. Authors throughout the country were churning out books on personal growth and self-esteem. Similar books had been around forever but not to my knowledge. Many of these books resided on the shelves of Overeaters Anonymous and The Institute for Advanced Pastoral Studies.

Was there even a library where we lived? I had no idea. The cares of life took up every minute of my day. There was no time for anything other than working in my cubicle and raising my two sons.

Now, when I wasn't at OA or the Institute, I was reading Napoleon Hill, Abraham Maslow, Carl Jung, Scott Peck, The Bhagavad Gita, Kahlil Gibran, Carlos Castaneda, Sri Aurobindo, and many others who left their imprint on my soul and expanded my awareness. Seminars and workshops were even more exciting than reading. Listening to someone tell a story made it come alive within me, and I never tired of learning. As time passed, something quite unexpected happened.

By the following year, I found myself hopelessly in love with Jack, the director of The Institute for Advanced Pastoral Studies. I learned firsthand why it is referred to as "falling" in love. Seemingly, I had absolutely no control or say in the matter. To my embarrassment, it also became obvious to everyone at IAPS how I felt about him.

In one workshop, I watched as Jack worked with a woman who had a lifelong reoccurring nightmare. She dreamed she was alone in a room with an open casket too terrified to look inside. Jack spent the better part of an hour talking her into moving about ten feet from where she was sitting to the imaginary casket. Finally, the woman approached the casket. As she peered in, her face beamed. The casket was filled with lighted candles. She turned, looked back at us, and smiled. In an instant, we all realized her lifelong nightmare had ended.

Perhaps Jack could do the same for me. It took this woman close to an hour to trust him enough to look into the casket. With Jack's guidance, I felt I could also trust him enough to enter that scary place again. Unfortunately, he never had time to repeat this meditation for me exclusively. Consequently, I could only theorize what the inside of that awful place might hold.

The more lectures I attended, the more significance this mysterious place assumed and the more I wanted to know where I had gone during that first meditation. However, I never again participated in Jack's guided meditations for fear of entering that place again and not being able to come back.

Everything he taught was new and exciting. There was no hell and damnation in any of his lectures or workshops.

In another workshop, Jack discussed sin and likened it to personality traits passed down from one generation to another. He explained this was the reason everyone was born into sin. It was exactly what I needed to hear for I'd wondered about this my whole life. To me it seemed so unfair to be born into sin. No one ever explained sin in terms of personality traits.

Another meaning of sin was simply "missing the mark." If a person had $1,000 but his goal was to have $2,000, he was missing the mark. Consequently, he was sinning. Sin took on far less significance than during my formative years. I reveled in this new way of looking at things that concerned me since I was a child.

IAPS introduced me to many spiritual teachers as well as their writings. I worked long hours into the night so I could spend every spare moment in this magical place.

At the weekly OA meeting, another new friend invited me to a church she said she enjoyed. It never occurred to me to attend a church other than a Lutheran Church, but I accepted.

After attending Jack Boland's Unity Church in Warren, Michigan, for the first time, I didn't want to leave. *The joy and happiness I felt after the service were indescribable.* This is how I had always pictured a church should be. One should feel better after spending an hour in church, any church, instead of dragging yourself out feeling like a useless rotten sinner—born in sin, living in sin and dying in sin. The uplifting, inspiring Unity message of joy and prosperity resonated with me. The Lutheran Church and its teachings of sin, hell, and damnation would never see me again.

Meanwhile, 20 pounds disappeared from my body while attending OA without even dieting. Just having people to talk to once a week helped enormously. I was deliriously happy and did not understand why. I felt radiant!

My parents noticed my transformation. My father, who hardly ever spoke to me except through my mother said, "Marie, I don't even know you anymore. You're a totally different person."

I smiled, amazed at his comment. "But Dad, this is the person who was inside the other one - I could never come out. This is the person I really am. I had to be this perfect wife, this perfect mother, this perfect everything—always striving to please everyone else and *never succeeding.* This is who I really am! Look at me Dad, I'm beautiful!" That scared the hell out of him, and he immediately reverted to his quiet self.

My mother, eyeing me suspiciously, said, "Marie, are you really as happy as you act or do you just think you are?"

I almost lost it after that remark. How could I possibly say to her, "Mom, you are what you think you are." How could she possibly understand?

14. A RADICAL CHANGE IN ATTITUDE

Weeks went by. My bliss continued in spite of the chaos in the house getting worse. Reflecting on my parents' remarks, I began wondering if there *was* something wrong with me. It didn't make sense to my logical mind to be this happy with everything around me falling apart. Perhaps this is how one felt going insane, although I was not aware of anyone in our family being insane.

I made an appointment for a physical to discuss my mental state with an internist. Of course, if I was going insane this was not something I wanted my own doctor to know so I chose a doctor I didn't know. After explaining my situation and many tests later, this doctor proclaimed me healthy and told me to go out and enjoy life. My acceptance of his prognosis lasted three days.

This doctor is only an internist, I thought to myself. *What does he know?* I decided to see the top psychiatrist at Beaumont Hospital. This was the doctor I had taken Rudy to when he had a nervous breakdown, after realizing his patented invention was not going to make him a millionaire overnight. If this psychiatrist was able to help Rudy, perhaps he could help me. More importantly, I met this doctor at his request during Rudy's therapy sessions. He already knew a lot of my background. My appointment was scheduled for the following week.

When I walked into his office, the doctor took one look at me and asked if I had a boyfriend? Remembering me from our previous consult, he saw my transformation. After I told him the reason for my visit, he too said, "Go be happy and enjoy your life," but not before asking me for the third time if I had a boyfriend. Even a brilliant psychiatrist is only a man, I suppose. This man could not imagine a woman being happy without a boyfriend. I was very disappointed with both the consult and his question.

15. FALLING IN LOVE

It was not until the following summer that Jack called me, and we began our unrequited love affair. By this time, I was painfully aware that several women at IAPS also were in love with him. A few months into our relationship, I told him that I did not want to be part of his adoring fan club. I was interested in a serious relationship leading to marriage. He never gave me an answer. Regardless of the emptiness I felt, eventually I realized that I had become a member of his club by continuing to spend time at the Institute.

One summer morning, Jack and I arrived in the parking lot of Cranbrook House at the same time. As he turned into the parking lot, he saw me and waved. We got out of our cars and exchanged pleasantries. Suddenly, I found myself somewhere else while standing in front of him. I "saw" gold flecks come down and surround us in waves of pulsing light. These waves swirled around us until we disappeared and became part of the pulsing light.

A feeling of pure love came over me. It was not a feeling of loving or even being loved. We were not discussing anything romantic. Yet, when those gold flecks enveloped us, I felt this incredible love. I was the object.

If God is love, then I experienced myself *as* God. I was infinite love and realized there is no death. Death is an illusion. I could have died for this man or anyone else for that matter. The pulsing light lasted for quite a while. Slowly, the gold flecks dissolved, and Jack came back into view.

15. FALLING IN LOVE

I looked up at him. He was still talking. *"Did you see that?"* I interrupted.

"What?" he asked.

"Those gold flecks swirling around us."

"No," he answered, looking at me strangely.

"Well, was there a break in our conversation?" I asked anxiously.

"What was the last thing you said to me?"

"We were surrounded by gold flecks for a very long time, Jack. How could you not see that?"

Quickly, I described what happened to me. In a matter of fact manner, he said, "Oh, it's just another experience. Forget it. Don't get attached to it."

He seemed impatient as we headed toward the Institute. Trying to keep up with him, I wondered why I felt so hurt. … This was the most amazing experience!

Forget it? Don't get attached to it?

I was disappointed and somehow sad with his response. His answers to my questions were always so profound. They felt true in my very soul. He not only answered my questions but rephrased them better than I originally posed them. By invalidating my experience, he also invalidated me. As much as I adored him, a little bit of me died that day.

These simple words describe my experience:

> *We stood and talked in quiet voice*
> *One lazy summer morning*
> *And as I watched his cradling smile*
> *It was not with eyes I saw*
> *When we became the dance of light*
> *I touched the face of God*

A couple of years later on a plane while I was reading Fritjof Capra's *The Tao of Physics*, I came across a much more eloquent description of his similar experience. He wrote:

"Being a physicist, I knew that the sand, rocks, water, and air around me were made of vibrating molecules and atoms, and that these consisted of particles which interacted with one another by creating and destroying other particles. I knew also that the earth's atmosphere was continually bombarded by showers of "cosmic rays," particles of high energy undergoing multiple collisions as they penetrated the air. All this was familiar to me from my research in high-energy physics, but until that moment, I had only experienced it through graphs, diagrams, and mathematical theories. As I sat on that beach my former experience came to life; I "saw" cascades of energy coming down from outer space, in which particles were created and destroyed in rhythmic pulses; I "saw" the atoms of the elements and those of my body participating in the cosmic dance of energy; I felt its rhythm and I "heard" its sound, and at that moment I knew that this was the Dance of Shiva, the Lord of Dancers worshiped by the Hindus."

And much later, I came across this verse, "St. Paul," by F.W.H. Myers:

> *Oh could I tell, ye surely would believe it!*
> *Oh could I only say what I have seen!*
> *How can I tell, or how can ye receive it,*
> *How, till he bringeth you where I have been?*

Actually, over the next two and a half years, Jack and I spent very little time together. He fit me in between "important" meetings and was always in a hurry. We rarely had a whole hour to ourselves. Even though I loved him, it

15. FALLING IN LOVE

was a very painful, lonely time for me. With Jack as with my husband, I was always on page ten, never important enough to be on page one. My whole world revolved around this man. For him, it seemed I was just another addition to his fan club.

One day when my mother was visiting at my house, she answered the doorbell. Jack had no time to introduce himself to her. Instead, he ran around her to get to the downstairs workroom where he knew I would be. A few minutes later after he left, my mother remarked, "He's very good looking." Looks to her had always been of great importance. For me, not so much anymore. At this point in my life, how I was treated took priority over looks. I graduated from judging a man by his looks during my marriage with Rudy. Marrying a good-looking man did absolutely nothing but make me miserable.

Jack did not spend enough time with me for either one of us to get to know the other. His idea of going to lunch was sitting on the floor at IAPS, sharing a banana and a handful of nuts. At first, even this seemed romantic to me. However, all those personal growth and self-esteem workshops were beginning to have an effect on me.

As I watched couples in church and elsewhere, it left me wanting a whole lot more than what Jack was offering. He had no time to support me during the many months it took to get my divorce. Settling the financial business of the house took even longer than the divorce. With my parents pretty much out of the picture, I was left to fend for myself. By now, I should have been used to going it alone. However, it would have been nurturing to have one other human being to talk to, but Jack was busy saving the world. He had no time to save me - not that I needed saving. All I wanted was someone to listen to me. Jack spent a lot of time listening to, and counseling clergy from around the country. *Listening* was part of his job. Had he done the same for me, it would have meant the world to me. ...

Sadly, it became even more apparent how unsatisfactory my relationship was with Jack after my son Kurt decided not to live with me, and I found myself alone in my five bedroom house.

I stopped going to IAPS and tried to make a life for myself. Now in my early forties, I had never even been on a "real" date with anyone other than my husband and that was at the age of 16. Uncomfortable as I found the experience, I forced myself to go out and meet new people.

A new elegant restaurant had opened in Southfield called Duglass-Duglass. The restaurant held Happy Hour each day starting at 4:00 p.m. There was also a dance floor about the size of a postage stamp and a trio playing music for people who wanted to get to know each other while dancing, rather than at the bar drinking.

As I threw on my dark blue A-line skirt and knit sweater, I sternly told God, "I'm going into this restaurant for 15 minutes even though I know I won't meet anyone."

As if God cared. Well, God must have smiled that afternoon and said, "I can do it in one minute."

As soon as I entered the restaurant, my new friend Pat waved me over to join her. "Hi Maria, I'd like you to meet Bob." Bob and I talked into the evening and then he asked me out. I accepted and so began my second relationship after my divorce.

Meanwhile, Jack realized I was not coming back to the Institute and that our relationship such as it was had ended. When he went to California on vacation with his children, he actually took the time to think about our relationship, while I did nothing *but* think about how miserable I felt in this relationship.

It was impossible to stay in a situation where I felt used. Twenty plus years of feeling used by Rudy was more than enough. To have Jack treat me so shabbily and throw

15. FALLING IN LOVE

a few crumbs my way when it was convenient for him hurt too much.

Jack did not even have time to propose to me in person. Instead, he wrote me a letter from California—another humiliation. I was not important enough to have him propose in person. When I turned him down, he actually had the nerve to be angry. I guess he forgot when I proposed to him earlier, he had not even bothered to give me a *no*.

After he got over his initial anger, he sent me the following poem. It was the first, last, and only time he told me he loved me. For me, however, it was much too late.

Maria

What wisdom does she possess
To deny herself and me
The fruit of our love?

I wish I knew
I do not want to know

Having exhausted all possibilities
I give up, abandon the quest
And feel, incredibly,
A deep peace

I love her more than I could ever say
Too painful to recount the ways
I love her

The closer I came, the more she fled
Repeating rationalizations
Never disclosing, never knowing
The sad script she must play out
The secret wisdom she acted out

> God, is the suffering really worth
> Whatever it is supposed to be worth?
>
> Love – Jack

Jack didn't know me at all. How could he? We spent so little time together. Had we married, the marriage would not have lasted a month. The fact that I will always love him has nothing to do with marriage. Somehow, I knew and had enough self-awareness to realize that a marriage would never have worked. *No,* was my greatest gift to him.

However, when I told Jack that I met someone else, and I wanted to see where it would lead, he did not believe me. He wrote me another letter accusing me of lying.

Instead of simply saying *you are lying* or *I don't believe you*, it took him a whole paragraph to accuse me of lying to him. "You are headstrong and not above falsifying reality a bit, to pretend you are getting what you want," and on and on.

While it definitely impressed and amused me, it also annoyed me simultaneously. How could anyone use so many words to say something so simple? There was no reason to defend myself or try to convince him otherwise. Feeling disappointed and sad, I folded his letter and stuck it in a drawer. Jack didn't even know me well enough to know that I would never lie to him.

16. LIFE AFTER DIVORCE

My thoughts turned to the new chapter about to open in my life. In spite of my deep feelings for Jack, I was hoping to stop the constant pain with a new relationship.

As it turned out, Bob and I were inseparable for almost three years. He owned his own production company, and with him, I learned about a completely new class of people. His company's numerous accounts included GM and many of the GM subsidiaries. Bob spent a great deal of his time entertaining GM executives, often on the golf course. He introduced me to golf, and I introduced him to tennis.

I had never been on a golf course much less played on one. The first time I rode onto the golf course with Bob, it was breathtaking with lush green grass, beautifully pruned trees, and sometimes even a glorious pond. What stillness with only the sounds of nature and such beauty! I was in awe—it felt spiritual. Forget playing golf, just driving around in the cart was heavenly. We spent many weekends on some of the most exquisite golf courses in Michigan.

Bob's company provided a yearly luxury vacation for the top sales people from around the country at posh golf resorts. This all-expenses-paid vacation was something these GM sales people looked forward to and worked toward throughout the year. A lot of organizing went into choosing the resort, planning the activities, even the prizes given out at the end of each golf game. Bob was involved in every detail. He even researched and designed the logo for the business card for this program. It was an easy project for him. While Bob put himself through school on a football scholarship, he also was offered an art scholarship at the same time.

When Bob saw how much I enjoyed golf, he bought me a beautiful set of golf clubs. What a difference these clubs made from playing with my Patty Berg beginner's set. I practiced for hours using only the pitching wedge. My subdivision did not allow fences so I could easily hit balls from my backyard to the neighbor's and back again. As with everything else in my life, I focused and put a lot of work into learning the game. Pitching a 100 golf balls was never enough. Often I counted 500 practice shots. At about 500, my shoulders began to ache.

By the second year, I was able to transfer my swing to all the other clubs and keep up with Bob and the other two guests he invited to make up our foursome. We enjoyed each other both on and off the golf course.

Sometime during the third year, our relationship had run its course. During one of our conversations, Bob let slip he was not interested in marriage. He wanted a weekend and vacation girlfriend. I, on the other hand, did not want to be a weekend and vacation girlfriend.

A few weeks later, Bob was surprised when I told him I was leaving Michigan. "How can you leave when we have been so close?" he asked.

"How close have we been, Bob?" I responded. "You just got through telling me that you are not interested in marriage. Do you really think I'm going to continue like this?"

Observing his reaction, I had the distinct impression this man did not believe I could give up our relationship so easily—the lifestyle, golf outings, vacations, and lovely jewelry.

Is disbelieving women a commonality among men? Is this trait in their genes? I wondered. Rudy had not believed I was divorcing him, Jack had not believed I met someone else,

16. LIFE AFTER DIVORCE

and now Bob did not believe I was leaving, not only him, but Michigan.

However, compared to "firing God" which I consider the most monumental act I'd ever accomplished, along with turning down Jack's proposal when I absolutely adored him, leaving Bob was a piece of cake. As far as all the perks were concerned, I was not attached to any of it.

During the years with Bob, I continued working full time on orthodontic study models to support myself in my very large home. As soon as my house sold, I sent out notices to all my accounts that I was taking a three-month hiatus starting at the end of the month.

I remember one orthodontist calling me. "Maria, what are you doing? I've never taken a three-month vacation in my life," he said.

Well, Dr. Shipko," I answered, "I've never had a vacation in 20 years so now I'm taking all those missed vacations in one lump sum."

Actually, I planned on taking a whole year off. Surely, a year would help me figure out what I wanted to do with my life. The doctor was not happy about having to find another source to process his study models.

My hope was *never* to return to processing study models, but I could not tell him that when he called. I needed time to figure out how I was going to support myself—how to set myself free from what had been my self-imposed but necessary prison in my home. Continuing the same line of work only in a different cubicle and adding more calluses on my palms was not something I wanted to do for the rest of my life.

My mother, bless her, allowed me to store all my equipment and my workbenches in her basement. She lived alone since my father's death a few years earlier. My siblings,

Susan and Johnny, had moved out long ago to raise their own families. Mother and I enjoyed each other's company when I stayed with her. One of her bedrooms was designated Marie's room. So, I brought a few accessories with me from my West Bloomfield home along with my clothes, and even transferred my phone number to a phone I had installed in her basement.

It was great staying with her, very different from when I was growing up. She loved waiting on me, and I loved being waited on. What a change for me!

One day I said to her jokingly, "No wonder Rudy didn't want a divorce. He didn't miss me. He missed not having a slave to wait on him, having been waited on his whole life."

No response from her. She just rolled her eyes and smiled. Even though my mother stopped me whenever I attempted to help her with the housework, she never stopped giving me advice.

Besides her "scripting" she was fond of saying, "Marie, I don't want to tell you what to do 'but', and then she proceeded to tell me what to do. "Mom," I told her laughing, "I'm going to put the word 'but' on your tombstone."

Yet, I never tired of listening to her advice, which as a teenager I couldn't stand. She always sounded so serious as if she had given this advice a great deal of thought. There was a kind of gentle humor in it, and for the most part, I dismissed it. Nevertheless, I was very much aware the advice was given in a spirit of love. The time I spent with her now in some small way compensated for all the years both my parents had been absent from my life when I was raising my children and working in my cubicle.

Now, my mother made it possible for me to take time off from all the responsibilities of life. There was an inner calmness not having to answer to anyone, not trying to please anyone, free of work and responsibilities. Not being

16. LIFE AFTER DIVORCE

dehumanized or called names anymore agreed with me. I relished every moment with her.

Being able to fill my mind with thoughts I chose instead of thoughts I *had* to think about was a wonderful gift in itself. Not having to worry about whether Ernst was going to have an asthma attack that day, how I was going to hide him if he did have an attack, keeping the house clean, getting the laundry done, preparing the meals for the family, making sure the study models were finished, packed, and ready to be shipped, keeping the electronic air purifier clean for Ernst, digging up sprinklers when they stopped working, painting the garage floor a battleship-gray once a year, cleaning the gutters, and on and on. It was great not being in a constant hyper-vigilant state expecting the next emergency to happen any minute and always being ready to spring into action. I'd never experienced such freedom. Even my breathing became calmer.

Perhaps during the next year, answers would reveal themselves. What I knew for sure was, after Bob, I lost all interest in another relationship. Dating did not appeal to me. Dating always seemed to revolve around eating and drinking, usually after 6:00 p.m.

West Bloomfield and the surrounding affluent towns and villages had the best restaurants one could possibly wish for. All were filled to capacity every evening. Yet, I never enjoyed sitting for two to three hours eating and drinking in any one of them. Drinking always gave me a headache and eating especially after 6:00 p.m. only exacerbated my weight problem. For as long as I can remember, my routine was up at 4:00 a.m. and to bed by 9:00 p.m.

The end of the month arrived ever so quickly. I shipped the last boxes of study models to the orthodontists and closed my business. A new chapter in my life was unfolding. I entered it with an open heart and great expectations.

17. THE "JOY" OF TRAVELING

My first of many trips began in Jenson Beach, Florida. The Inn where I was staying offered fishing charters for their guests. So, I decided to give it a try and joined five other guests from the Inn on *Cameron's Charter Fishing*, for this adventure. In spite of my concerns about getting seasick, things went surprisingly well. Call it beginner's luck or whatever, over a five hour period, I managed to catch three beautiful sailfish. One of the other guests helped me reel them in. Not having the heart to kill such beautiful creatures, I tagged them with my name and sent them on their way. All six of us caught an assortment of fish, as well as several more sailfish, but I was the only person who caught three sailfish.

On the way back to the Inn, Captain Cameron told me that catching three sailfish in one day was a record. After he docked the boat, he handed me a certificate with my name on it, next to a colorful picture of a sailfish. He congratulated me, and signed it to make it official. I couldn't help but wonder how many certificates he really handed out. In any case, the fishing experience was memorable.

The following week, my Irish girlfriend Jane and her sister Emily drove down from West Bloomfield and stayed with me for a while. Being from Belfast, Ireland, they both had these wonderful Irish brogues which I enjoyed listening to, especially when they bickered with each other. Jane was a self-employed hairdresser and Emily a homemaker. Jane loved golf as much as I did, and back in West Bloomfield we played at least once or twice a week on nearby local courses.

17. THE "JOY" OF TRAVELING

Jane wasn't interested in playing golf since her sister didn't play. However, when I told her about my fishing excursion, and showed her my "official" certificate, they both decided to go on this adventure.

This time I didn't worry about getting seasick, and enjoyed myself much more than I had during my first outing. Jane and Emily each caught a sailfish but didn't want to keep them, so they tagged and released them. All three of us caught several large king mackerel, which my two friends decided to have processed and smoked to take back home with them. For me, the fishing wasn't a priority. It was much more fun watching Jane and Emily having a good time, rather than catching any more fish. ...

Every day was a "fun" day for us, regardless of what we did, whether it was having lunch while watching other tourists, shopping, enjoying the beach and the salt water air, or trying on our new bathing suits. We never ran out of stories to share, and really enjoyed each other's company. Talking definitely was something the three of us delighted in, non-stop. The time they spent with me was precious.

All too soon, the two sisters said goodbye, and headed back to West Bloomfield, with their smoked mackerel. This was the last time I saw Jane, although many years later we did talk once on the phone. I could easily have hitched a ride back to my mother's. Instead, I decided to fly straight from Florida to New Orleans to visit my cousin Linda, whom I had not seen in years.

It happened to be Mardi Gras season in New Orleans. There were endless parties daily from morning through night. During the Bacchus celebration, thousands of people lined the streets as 23 floats and numerous bands passed by. The theme this year was Rivers of the World. Each float represented a river from different parts of the world. The floats were exquisite, from the Nile in Egypt, Yukon in

Canada, Seine in Paris, the Amazon in Brazil, to our own Mississippi.

The first float had Kirk Douglass sitting on his throne reigning as Bacchus, Greek god of Wine, tossing out doubloons, beads, gaudy plastic jewelry, and toys. All of it was new to me. There was no room in my suitcase to pack the shoebox of mementos I caught from passing floats. Not wanting to offend Linda by tossing it in the trash, I mailed it to my mother back in Michigan. She could toss it in the trash for me.

Next, I decided to spend a few weeks in Mexico, and it made sense to me to leave from Linda's instead of returning to my mother's home. Linda was horrified when I told her. She apparently called her mother in Lake Forest, Illinois, and between the two of them, they were certain I was going to be murdered or worse in Mexico. As it turned out, they convinced me that going on a cruise was a much safer trip for me. Never having been on a cruise, I didn't object. So, I booked the cruise out of Miami and flew there directly from New Orleans.

When I boarded the ship in Miami, I discovered approximately 800 women on board. They also must have concluded that a cruise would be a safe vacation.

This ten-day cruise was the worst of my trips. Thank goodness, I met a Chicago police officer named Caroline who ended up being my roommate. There were four of us in our cabin. After listening to the two other women argue all night, Caroline and I were lucky enough to be assigned to another cabin. We shared our stories and enjoyed each other's company. Caroline received a prize for being the youngest grandmother on board at the age of 37. This turned out to be the highlight of our cruise. There was not much to do on this ship other than eat and play bingo.

Contrary to the TV commercials which showed couples dancing and having a blast, there were no unattached men,

17. THE "JOY" OF TRAVELING

only hundreds of women. The few men who were dancing all came with their girlfriends or wives. There would be no dancing for Caroline and me. Caroline was not too keen on dancing with me. Swimming was out. The pool was under repair and had no water in it. The cruise consisted of 14 meals a day and bingo. Both Caroline and I disliked bingo.

How much better would *The Song of Norway* cruise ship have been? That ship was my first choice, but when I attempted to book passage, every cabin was already taken. This "fun" ship was the only ship with available space.

As fate would have it, both cruise ships docked in San Juan, Puerto Rico. Passengers from both ships were herded into very lovely, expensive shops and great restaurants. Looking around in one of the shops, we met two women from *The Song of Norway*. Anxiously, I asked the women how they were enjoying themselves, and what was happening on their ship. Their ship turned out to be a duplicate of ours, with the majority of passengers being women, all feeling safe no doubt.

At the end of the cruise, Caroline and I each were eight pounds heavier. We exchanged phone numbers and addresses, and promised to stay in touch. I never heard from Caroline. I would never go on another cruise, either alone or with someone. Whenever I see the "fun" cruise commercial, I begin yelling at the TV, then end up laughing at myself for believing the commercial in the first place.

A few months earlier, during my first charter fishing trip in Jensen Beach, I met a woman who had free airfare to anywhere in the United States. Her sister worked for one of the airlines, and this was a benefit offered to the families of their employees. At the time, we discussed perhaps taking a trip together. To me, the destination was irrelevant, as long as it wasn't another cruise.

When I called her, she immediately suggested Hawaii. I agreed and we made plans to meet in Los Angeles within

OUT OF TRANSYLVANIA

two weeks. In the meantime, I returned to my mother's in Michigan, where I starved myself trying to lose weight.

Regardless of how hard I tried, those eight pounds simply would not come off. I had no choice but to pack larger clothes, which were never as cute as my smaller sizes. I left from Detroit Metro for Los Angeles to meet up with Sandy still feeling fat from the cruise. She made all the arrangements for us, which I really appreciated, and we flew to Hawaii from Los Angeles.

Sandy, a divorced woman in her late thirties without children, and apparently not having to work, was free to do a lot of traveling, especially with free airfare. However, like me she was not crazy about traveling alone. ...

During the flight, Sandy shared that she did not play golf, so after arriving and settling in at our hotel, I went down to the desk and made reservations to play golf the following day. Sandy planned on exploring the local shops and tourist attractions.

On the golf course, the following morning, the club paired me with three others, a married couple from the Los Angeles area and a local gentleman named Charles. Charles was my partner and at the end of the game, he offered me a guest pass to his private club, the Outrigger Canoe Club. When I told him I had a girlfriend with me, he said that he didn't mind if I invited her. He was certain we would both enjoy ourselves there. Charles was married, and there were no strings attached to his most generous offer. In fact, we never saw the man during all the time Sandy and I spent at this lovely club.

Sandy was thrilled! By the third day at the Outrigger, it became obvious she did not want me around. I reminded her that she was there because I invited her. Charles had given the guest pass to me and not to her.

Sandy, had a long T-shirt with a huge portrait of Tom Selleck on the front. She wore this shirt turned inside out

17. THE "JOY" OF TRAVELING

to bed every night. The only thing Sandy wanted to do was search for Tom Selleck, who I discovered later spent a lot of time at this club.

Sandy never tired of searching for the TV star. What in the world would she have done had he shown up at the Outrigger? Selleck, never appeared, but Sandy was happy spending her time on the lookout for him. Within days we discovered that we had very little in common.

My lifelong habit was early to bed and early to rise, the opposite of Sandy's. She did not accompany me to the golf course, and I did not join her in the bar in the evening. To Sandy, I was probably a total bore since I do not smoke, do not drink, and sure as heck am not interested in casual sex. For me, golf, swimming, sunbathing, and thinking were more than enough.

Lying on the beach, my mind was occupied with thoughts of how I was going to support myself. How was I going to make a living by doing something I enjoyed, something that did not create calluses on my hands? My mother's scripting, "Don't expect a man to pay your rent" was so deeply embedded in my psyche that although I had numerous opportunities to get involved with very wealthy men, I dismissed each without even consideration. I was determined to "pay my own rent" and not answer to anyone.

At the end of each week, we kept extending our stay in our hotel. After four extensions, I had enough of the Outrigger Canoe Club. Their lunches were wonderful, but I had to exercise restraint. Those eight pounds I gained on the cruise could easily turn into 10 and 12. By the fourth week my skin was so tanned from being on the golf course and sunbathing, I could hardly recognize myself in the mirror.

During the fifth week, I let Sandy know that I couldn't take any more fun, and thought it was time to settle our tab so we could leave. The manager gave me our invoice for all the lunches, drinks, and services we had used during the time we spent there. I added it up and handed the bill to Sandy, circling her half of the total amount. Sandy told me she did not want to be bothered now, but would send Charles a check for her portion to the Outrigger Canoe Club. This was not acceptable to me, and I was not happy with her decision.

The last thing I was going to do was shortchange this very generous man, who had put his complete trust in me by offering me the use of his club. The fact that she was not willing to pay immediately set off alarm bells. How could I trust this woman, having known her for only a short period?

It turned out to be a standoff, with me refusing to allow her to use the guest pass Charles had given me. Sandy could stay at the hotel for as long as she wished because I was not leaving without her paying her share.

After a horrific argument, she finally handed over a check for her portion of our bill. I can only wonder if she stopped payment. Arguing, was not something I was good at, and doing so always had a negative effect on every cell in my body.

Sandy and I did not speak during the flight back to Los Angeles. We both knew there was not a chance in hell we could ever be friends.

Close to six months had passed since I began this travel adventure. The thought of spending another six months like this made me cringe. Every Holiday Inn is pretty much the same, regardless of whether it's in Detroit or Hawaii. The captain's announcement "fasten your seatbelts" jolted me out of my daydream.

Upon landing in Los Angeles, sitting and waiting for the commuter bus to our hotel, I realized that traveling was not my cup of tea.

17. THE "JOY" OF TRAVELING

I wondered if other people felt as useless as I did when they took vacations. Or, did they actually enjoy living out of a suitcase, going from one place to another, smoking, drinking, and partying?

When the gentleman next to me abruptly got up, he left part of his newspaper on the seat. Without even thinking, I reached over and picked it up.

It happened to be the Los Angeles classified ads. There, on the front page was an ad for someone experienced processing orthodontic study models. The strangest feeling came over me.

"This ad was meant for me!" My spirits lifted and I felt better, hoping this would end my meaningless traveling days. I looked forward to feeling useful again. At the hotel, Sandy and I parted ways. ... The only thing that interested me was this ad.

Wilson Dental Radiography & Photography in Van Nuys was looking for someone with experience in processing orthodontic study models. As far as I was concerned, there wasn't a person in the whole country with more experience processing dental casts than I was.

I answered the ad with great anticipation and confidence. After talking to the owner of the company, John Wilson hired me immediately to do a three-month marketing survey for him in Van Nuys, Los Angeles, and the surrounding areas. John wanted to know if the orthodontists who sent their patients for diagnostic X-ray surveys, were interested in his company also providing study model services. Adding study models would provide the orthodontists with a full service center.

Presently the doctors had to train people in their offices to do this plasterwork or take the impressions themselves, then pack and ship them to a number of different places for processing. Processing study models was also a very noisy, messy job with plaster dust everywhere. John felt that the orthodontists could benefit if he offered to provide everything under one roof, during the patients' initial appointments. To me, this was a great idea!

These X-ray facilities offered diagnostic dental X-rays, cephalometric X-rays with tracings, TMJ and dental implant tomography and dental photography, skills all orthodontists require in their practices. I knew at least 20 orthodontists back in Michigan who could use this service. Orthodontists where I didn't have to battle for an appointment, but could simply walk in and offer them my new skills. The more I thought about it, the more exciting the idea became.

During my interview, John told me about a company that rented out fully furnished executive apartments by the month within walking distance of his business. When my interview concluded, I walked down to this building and booked an apartment for three months.

The following Monday I reported for work at Wilson Radiography & Photography. As I made the rounds visiting his accounts to discuss the prospect of providing study model service, I became quite familiar with all phases of these dental imaging centers. The more I learned, the more they appealed to me. I reported regularly to John regarding my discussions with the orthodontists.

Three months later, after completing the survey, John asked me if I wanted to go to Dallas and set up a study model department at another Wilson Radiography & Photography facility he owned. I let him know how much I loved the concept of his imaging centers, wanted the training to run a center, and was ready, willing, and able to do whatever it took to accomplish this. John was open to the idea and agreed to help me in exchange for me going to Dallas.

17. THE "JOY" OF TRAVELING

His company enrolled me in the basic radiology course at UCLA while I flew back to Michigan to my mother's house, purchased a new car, packed several suitcases of clothing, and drove from Michigan to Dallas. The company had arranged for me to rent a furnished apartment in a very upscale area, close to the Wilson X-ray facility in Dallas.

For the next 15 months, I lived in Dallas, set up the model department, trained under supervision X-raying patients while studying basic radiology under a professor at UCLA. Wilson Radiography & Photography was paying me more money weekly, than my husband's and my combined income had been in West Bloomfield. At the same time they were teaching me a brand new skill I absolutely loved. I couldn't have been happier.

A few months after settling in, I discovered Dallas also had a Unity Church, which I attended regularly. Fifteen months flew by. ...

When I left Dallas, the model department was set up, I completed my hands-on X-ray training, passed my radiology exam at UCLA, and had a brand new X-ray license in my hand. These last 15 months were not only more fulfilling than any trip I had previously taken, I also added another skill to my repertoire. Thank you, Universe!

I was humbled when I reflected on how my so-called "lowly plasterwork" made possible acquiring these new skills. No more calluses! Not only was this work fun, it was by far the most lucrative of any profession I came across.

These imaging centers made more money for their owners than any dentist or orthodontist I ever met. Of the three owners I knew, two did not even work in their facilities. They had well-trained technicians running them. At that time, all the dental imaging centers throughout California were on a cash basis. Therefore, there were no third-party payments, which made life a whole lot easier. I did not know it at the time but I would eventually make more money in one day, in my own imaging center, than my now ex-husband made in a month. Of course, I never told him this. He would not have believed me because I could hardly believe it myself.

Another new world opened up to me. I was not only thrilled, but oh so grateful!

Wilson Dental Radiography & Photography then offered me a job in Pearl City, Hawaii. John was opening another imaging center. After much consideration, I decided not to move to Hawaii but rather accept a job running an imaging center in Walnut Creek, California, owned by a fellow in Sacramento. The owner had several X-ray facilities in Sacramento, and I spent a couple of months working there, before the owner and I commuted daily to his Walnut Creek Center, approximately 90 miles south of Sacramento.

When I felt comfortable enough to run the place by myself, I found a room to rent with an elderly lady in Walnut Creek, about two miles from my job. Daily, I honed my new skills and looked forward to going to work, which didn't seem like work at all. It seemed more like going to play. The more experience I accumulated, the sooner I would be able to return to West Bloomfield with my wonderful new skills.

After settling in my room and going to work became a routine, I asked myself, "Now what else am I here for?" That is how I came upon the Unity Church of Walnut Creek. Carol Knox was the senior minister there. Her church was filled to capacity each Sunday. When I met her and talked to her one-on-one for the first time, she asked me, "Why aren't you a minister?"

Smiling I replied, "Because I'm not interested in saving the world. The world was fine before I came into it and will be fine after I leave." "Why did *you* become a minister, Carol?" I asked her.

17. THE "JOY" OF TRAVELING

"Because I wanted to show off," she replied.

Really! That surprised me. "I guess I'm not interested in showing off either, but I do enjoy their classes. Ever since I fired that angry, vengeful God I grew up with, Unity has been a great blessing and joy to me."

During the week, I focused on becoming more and more adept at X-raying patients and managing the imaging center. On Sundays after watching Carol "perform" her sermon, I spent time at the Unity bookstore or participating in one of their many classes. If nothing was going on in the church, I took golf lessons in a beautiful 55-plus community called Rossmoor. They had two golf courses only a few minutes from where I lived, worked and attended Church.

On February 1, 1987, I arrived a few minutes late for church. Every seat was taken downstairs, so I ended up in the balcony. I barely had time to sit down when someone announced from the podium that Carol had just been shot and killed by a woman intruder at her home in Antioch. At first, the whole congregation sat speechless without making a sound for what seemed like an eternity. Finally, I got up, walked out in a daze, and drove home without talking to anyone.

About half an hour later, I drove back to the church to confirm what I heard earlier, not wanting to believe it was true. Unfortunately, it really was true. Most of the congregation was still outside the church discussing the shooting.

The following months were very difficult for the congregation and especially for Carol's family. Carol was only 48 years old when she was killed. In spite of this horrible event, I continued taking classes, even at Unity Village in Lee's Summit, Missouri, the headquarters for all the Unity churches throughout the country.

While living in California, I thought nothing of driving from one coast to the other. On one trip, I took the northern route through the mountains to spend time with my cousin

Maria in Lake Forest, Illinois, then on to my mother's in Royal Oak, Michigan. When I spent time at Unity Village, I took the middle route through Kansas and from there to my mother's in Michigan, then on to my cousin Sue's place in Tampa. When I drove straight to Tampa from California, I took the southern route and Highway 10. Usually these trips amounted to three to four days of non-stop driving. I drove the southern route at least four times. In those days it took me 18 hours of driving the first two days and 12 hours the third day for the southern route.

Thinking back on these long non-stop trips, I am amazed that I could stay awake that long. When staying at my cousin Sue's place in Tampa, I always attended Tampa Unity. I even taught a class there on "You Can Heal Your Life" based on Louise Hay's book by the same title.

I spent more than 20 years in Unity, accumulating enough credits to apply for the Unity Ministerial Program as well as the Unity Teachers Program. When traveling or visiting friends in other states, I always attended a Unity church.

Later on, I much preferred Science of Mind, the teachings of Ernest Holmes and The Church of Religious Science. Yet, regardless of how many New Thought churches I attended, there was always something missing for me. I could not quite articulate *what* was missing, however, I knew that none of the churches filled that void in me.

On one occasion, I was in a group of people preparing to take yet another class in a nearby church. I asked the minister if he had ever had a spiritual experience. "No", he replied.

As I sat down, I asked myself, "What in the world am I doing here?" This man could only teach me the church's rules, beliefs, and dogma. How could he explain *"vision"* to me or answer any of the questions I wondered about my whole life when he'd never had a spiritual experience? Yet, he was a very successful minister.

17. THE "JOY" OF TRAVELING

For the first time I saw churches as a business – *big* business in the case of this particular church. This minister was a super successful businessman, but had nothing to offer me in the way of spirituality or feeding my soul by putting my questions to rest. I decided not to take this class and lost interest in all the other classes offered. Eventually, I stopped attending all churches. Ah, but I'm getting ahead of my story.

18. MEETING NEVILLE

Sometime during 1997, I drove from Rossmoor in Walnut Creek to stay at my cousin Sue's place in Tampa. As usual, I attended Unity Church of Tampa while there.

One Sunday I was in charge of a book sale at the church. Hundreds of wonderful books were donated. I'd just finished reading Eric Butterworth's book, *The Universe Is Calling*, and Arnold Patten's, *You Can Have It All*.

I decided to play a game, actually more of a challenge, like when I gave God 15 minutes to find someone special for me at Duglass-Duglass. "Okay God, choose a book for me," I said aloud in a playful mood since I was the only one in the room. I knew He heard me, but I was still curious as to the outcome. However, I was not prepared for what happened, not in a million years.

Unity people love reading because, by the end of that sale, only a handful of books remained. Perhaps I had been foolish leaving it up to God. Perhaps I should have chosen a book when the opportunity was there. Nothing left on the table looked very interesting.

Then my eye caught this pathetic little frayed, tattered book. Even the color was awful. It wasn't brown and it wasn't beige. I didn't have a name for the awful color. As I picked it up, I wondered how anyone could choose such a terrible color for a book. Yet, I was drawn to it. I glanced at the back cover first and then turned it over. The title of the book read *The Law and the Promise* by Neville. The author used only one name.

18. MEETING NEVILLE

Curious and even a little anxious, I brought it home with me and began reading. There were only 156 pages so it didn't take me long to finish the book.

Wow! How is it that after reading hundreds of books, taking classes and workshops for years, not only at Unity but also from some of the top gurus in the country, I never heard of Neville? How is that possible?

I met Deepak Chopra in Sacramento when he was charging $29 for his lectures. Edgar Cayce's son Hugh Lynn taught me the process of forgiveness. Wayne Dyer often came to Unity in Warren, Michigan, in the early eighties. In Nathanial Brandon's, "Self-Esteem and the Art of Being" workshop, I discovered the child in me, held her, and loved her. The visions I had during Stan Grof's "Holotropic Breathing Class", are a book in themselves. In one vision, I saw myself on a cross while relatives were milling around below. Yet, despite so many years of lectures and workshops, not once did I hear the name *Neville* mentioned.

The next day I ordered his other nine books. This tattered little book would set me on a path where all my questions about God were answered. Neville's lectures also explained my visions during Stan Grof's Holotropic Breathing Class, and both the foreshadowing during my first guided meditation in 1979 at IAPS, as well as the golden pulsing waves of light surrounding Jack and me in the Cranbrook parking lot in 1980. Neville understood and validated my experiences through his lectures. He taught *"vision,"* since throughout his own life, he participated in hundreds of mystical experiences. Neville had the courage (which I sorely lacked) to enter those visions and explore them and then share them with the world. Neville's teachings would change my life.

Thank you, Universe! You have outdone yourself. What a gift! From that day on, Neville's teachings became my church.

No more searching. My search was over! I finally found my religion. Nothing was missing anymore.

After the book sale at Tampa Unity, I also met Reverend Roy Fox. When I told him of my scripting and constantly trying not to want so much, he smiled. Reverend Fox explained to me that the word *desire* actually contains two words, *de* meaning *of* and *sire* meaning *Father, of the Father*. He explained that desire or wanting was the Father calling me to come up higher.

"The Father never calls you to come lower," he added. "Desire in your heart is the *knocking at the door* referred to in scripture. God through desire speaks to you and is telling you that you already have what you desire. However, you have to use the *Law* to bring it into fruition. When you imagine without doubt, you already have what you desire, it will appear in the objective world. The world will then call it real. Never feel guilty for wanting or desiring something. Know <u>that</u> is God talking to you. *It is God in you desiring."*

Oh my, another gift showered on me! After all these years of trying to rein in and curb my desires, I was finally free of guilt. Not only was I free of guilt, but I could desire as much as I desired.

My desiring, however, took an unexpected path after meeting Neville. Another new adventure was unfolding in my life, an adventure of learning from the most profound spiritual teacher I have ever come across. When I met him in 1997, through his books, he went by only one name, Neville.

19. THE LAW ACCORDING TO NEVILLE

Neville was born in Barbados, West Indies, in 1905 to a large family of nine boys and one girl. As a child he was known as the mystical child in his family. At 17 he came to the United States to study drama, and earned a living as a dancer. In 1932, after meeting an Ethiopian Rabbi named Abdulah, he lost all interest in dancing and the theater. For the next five years he devoted all his time to the study of mysticism under the tutelage of Abdulah. Neville practiced what he learned from his teacher, and after testing his knowledge, when it became personal experience, he began lecturing in New York City and throughout the country to teach others.

Eventually Neville made his home in Los Angeles and lectured to thousands of people at the Wilshire Ebell Theater, the Fox Wilshire Theater and other theaters, as his audience skyrocketed. …

According to Neville, the Promise came before the Law. However, he had not yet experienced the Promise. During this time, he taught the Law while the Promise unfolded in him over many years. Neville said of his teacher Abdulah, "He knew more about Christianity than any person I have met in my life."

Neville was not a scholar. In fact, he never finished high school. He wrote about firsthand experience. His teachings came through revelations. Wow again! His books were like nothing I ever read. They electrified and thrilled me! His interpretation of the Bible spoke to me like no other book. His experience of scripture came alive in me. I hungered for his interpretations of the Word of God and understood Amos 8:11: "I will send a famine in the land, not a famine of bread, nor a thirst for water, but of hearing the words of the Lord."

This famine had come upon me and no church I ever attended satisfied this hunger until God handed me Neville's book *The Law and the Promise*. After all my searching for answers, for the first time the stories of scripture made sense to me. This religion agreed with me. I did not have to work at believing his teachings. I *knew* he taught truth.

Neville spent six to seven hours a day studying the Bible and lectured for more than 30 years. I never tire of hearing his interpretation of the Bible, and for several years, I spent six or seven hours a day listening to his lectures, and many more hours on weekends. Some lectures I memorized by listening to them so often. At times, my legs become numb from not moving for so many hours. "All knowledge (science), will eventually pass away," he said. "Wisdom (revealed truth), is forever."

The Law as Neville taught consists of three steps:

1. Desire
2. Physical immobility
3. Imagining - by assuming the *feeling* of the wish already fulfilled.

   That is, "Thinking <u>From</u> the end, not <u>Of</u> the end," which simply means *not looking at* your imagined vision (picture in your mind), but stepping into the vision and participating *from* it.

From Neville's lectures, I learned the cause of the phenomena of life. How things happen. From him I learned the technique of imagining a desire into existence. There is nothing more exciting than imagining a desire into existence.

19. THE LAW ACCORDING TO NEVILLE

The whole of life is trying to appease hunger or desire. To assume your desire is already fulfilled without doubting is the means of manifesting your desire. It is your certainty that you already possess what you desire that makes it appear in your world. The process happens so naturally that at first you *always* say to yourself, "Oh, that would have happened anyway."

God never stops calling me to want more. I also understand that my mother did not know the Law and its operation. She was only trying to keep me from being hurt and disappointed by telling me not to want so much. Oh, if she had only known Neville's teachings. Of course, she would have disagreed vehemently, when I explained to her that she is actually a Jew. *We are all Jews.*

When I was growing up, I often said to her, "Mom, I feel Jewish." I can still "hear" that *serious* voice of hers, asking me, "Bast dau tierich?" in Saxon, which is "Bist du verrückt?" in German, and "Are you crazy?" in English. That was always her response, whenever, I said something she considered "outrageous". Now, here was Neville lecturing:

"You cannot be a Christian without also being a Jew. Judaism is the foundation, the Old Testament, the tree. Christianity is its fulfillment, the New Testament, the apple. You can have a tree, (be a Jew without an apple). However, you cannot have an apple, (be a Christian without a tree.) The Old and New Testament are hyphenated, Judeo-Christian, and are one book."

Yet, as much as I reveled in my *knowing* the Law, I also understood that knowing without doing is worthless. As William Shakespeare said in *The Merchant of Venice.*

"If to do were as easy as to know what were good to do, chapels had been churches, and poor men's cottages princes'

palaces. It is a good divine that follows his own instructions: I can easier teach twenty what were good to be done, than be one of the twenty to follow mine own teaching."

It took a while for the knowing to take root. Meanwhile, there were numerous side trips where I became lost in the activities of Caesar's world. I spent many years fulfilling my mother's first scripting, "Never expect a man to pay your rent." My wonderful X-ray business in California enabled me to retire at the age of 56, four years earlier than I had planned.

Retirement, (after selling my X-ray business) was my gift to myself, for being a workaholic since the age of 12. Retirement also allowed me the luxury of spending my time as I wished, live wherever I wanted, and even travel when I chose to. ...

My final destination, however, was predetermined. "For He chose us in Him before the foundation of the World." Ephesians 1:4. The destination of every man born of woman was, is, and always will be God! There is nothing but God. For me, the doing, the testing, began in Rossmoor, Walnut Creek, California.

Here I played at retirement on the golf course, the tennis courts, and the swimming pools in Rossmoor. At the same time, I was keenly aware of the hunger in my soul calling me to come up higher.

Both Neville and William Blake taught that human imagination is God. Imagination is the creative power responsible for everything in the objective world. This is a Law or Universal Principle. This Law governs every man and woman regardless of whether you know it or not. As William Blake said:

> *"<u>Imagination creates reality,</u>*
> *Man is all imagination,*
> *God is Man and exists in us and we in Him.*

19. THE LAW ACCORDING TO NEVILLE

*The Eternal Body of Man is the Imagination,
That is, God, Himself."*

Saying this is easy enough, however, knowing it from experience is quite another tale. The wonderful part about this Law is that you do not have to believe it. You can test the Law yourself—anyone can test it. Costs you nothing. Results will show you if it is true.

2 Corinthians 13:5 (English translation) *Examine yourselves, to see whether you are in the faith. <u>Test yourselves</u>. Or do you not realize this about yourselves that Jesus Christ is in you? Unless indeed you fail to meet the test!*

The first test is so simple. If, when you hear the word God, Lord, Jehovah, Father, Jesus, Christ, etc., and your mind travels to something or someone outside yourself, you have the wrong God. *You have to first believe that God exists inside of you.*

While the test is simple enough, it took a lifetime to get past the *misinterpretations* I grew up with as taught in the churches. These churches, even today, teach of a God outside one's Self.

Although the memory of my relationship with God goes back to the age of five, all those years even into adulthood, God was always in the passenger seat while I was driving. When He finally moved to the driver's seat within me, only then did the stories in scripture begin to make sense. Neville's interpretation of scripture showed me the way to move from innocence to experience; from the belief in an external historical Jesus or God, to a divine indwelling God of experience.

Only then did I learn that spirituality is the gradual transition from a traditional God outside myself to a God within me. Through Neville's teachings, I learned God does not work for me but through me. I am the operant power.

There is no one outside myself doing anything to me or for me, regardless of my behavior.

No wonder God never answered my prayers. The God I prayed to was somewhere outside of me. Real prayer is not petitioning. Real prayer is giving thanks for already having what you want. The God I fired and had taken so seriously is nonexistent. The Grace I experienced after firing that external, nonexistent God, is the real God in action, God's gift of Himself to me inside of me – the *real* God, the *only* God, the "I AM" within me. And, I did not know it at the time. I did not know then, God is known by experience or not at all.

Slowly I moved from knowing the Law to testing the Law *consciously. I wanted to prove to myself that my imagination creates my reality, and to discover for myself the creative power, the "I AM" within me.*

20. TESTING THE LAW

In 2004, after spending a year in Florida, I returned to Rossmoor. I purchased the identical condo I sold the previous year, on the same street one entry higher on the hill, and began remodeling the unit.

At this point in my life, I was familiar with Neville's teachings for seven years. Practicing his teachings consistently, however, was not an obsession for me at this time. Even though I was aware of the Law that governs everyone's life knowingly or unknowingly, it was not until I discovered his lectures on YouTube that his teachings consumed my life.

Presently, I found myself remodeling another unit in Rossmoor with the intention of furnishing it to be identical to my previous condo, not wanting to spend a lot of time being settled. It was much easier to purchase identical furniture, the identical kitchen and bathroom tile, knowing I liked the way my previous unit looked.

Two women I met in Rossmoor recommended a handyman to redo the tile in the kitchen. This handyman gave me lists of materials he needed and then a separate price for his work. While he was working, I went out and purchased the items on his list.

Almost from day one, I believed the man was stealing from me. To prove to myself that this was true, I set a trap for him. I placed four bags of grout that he had me purchase on the floor, and then left him alone in my home.

When I returned later that afternoon, there were only three empty bags on the floor. When I asked him where the fourth bag was, he told me he'd put it in his van in order to return it to the store. Trying to stay calm and politically correct, I said, "Well, let's get the grout, and I will return it myself." When he opened the van door, next to the grout sat an unopened box of tile—tile he had stolen from me the previous day. Without saying a word, he transferred both to my car.

I then called the two women who had recommended him. No, they were not aware that he stole anything from them. After contemplating this for a long time, I asked myself, *"Where was this thief?"* This man played the part of a thief, exactly as I imagined. Had this man played this part *because* that is how I saw him in my imagination? If imagination creates reality, the answer is a definite YES! At first, this was difficult to accept, but my searching for answers only intensified.

From then on, I began paying more attention to my thoughts—my inner speech. When meeting people, I deliberately practice imagining positive traits about them, regardless of their appearance, and first outer impressions.

At about the same time, my next experience with this Law transpired. One day I decided to shop for a dress at Nordstrom. Unlike most of my friends, the prospect of spending hours looking through all those racks did not appeal to me. Actually, I dislike shopping. Instead, I approached the nearest salesgirl and described the kind of dress I wanted. Of course, in the back of my mind what I really wanted was a dress that made me appear five inches taller and 20 pounds lighter. In my imagination I "saw" a simple black dress, V-neck, long sleeves, preferably A-line, with mid-calf length. The salesgirl said, "We have nothing like that in here right now."

Then I noticed the dress she was wearing. "That dress," I said, pointing to her. "Where did you buy that dress?"

"Why, here at Nordstrom," she replied.

20. TESTING THE LAW

"That is exactly what I want, only in black. Do you mind if I ask how much you paid for it?"

"Three hundred dollars," she replied.

"It's perfect! Can I order it?"

"Oh no, this dress is over two years old," she said. "We would not be carrying this anymore. I'm so sorry."

"Are you sure," I asked.

"Yes," she replied. "We constantly get new styles and our inventory has a quick turnover. There is no use even checking with other stores. None would have a two-year-old dress in stock."

Disappointed, I thanked her and headed for the escalator. The image of that perfect dress kept dancing around in my head as I headed for the parking lot. That's it! I want that dress. I am willing to waste the day driving out to San Leandro to the Nordstrom Outlet Store.

What a crazy idea, I thought to myself. It didn't matter. I was going to do it anyway. The 45 minute drive one way was worth it to me, and all the way I "saw" that dress in the store, in my imagination.

Arriving at the store, I went straight to the designer section and began rummaging through the black dresses with fierce determination. In less than five minutes, to my utter amazement, there was the identical dress the salesgirl had on, in black, V-neck, long sleeves, A-line, mid-calf length. Even on the hanger, the vertical knit ribbing from below the bust to slightly below the hips had a slenderizing effect. Hastily, I glanced at the label—size eight, exactly what I wanted. The price was $59.99. Without trying it on, I paid for it and headed for my car. Unbelievable! How could this be?

What Do You Want? This is the most implied question throughout the Bible. Know what you want. I wanted the dress the salesgirl had on in my size in black, instead of her wine color. That is exactly what I got. *But, how could it be that simple*, I asked myself?

I will share another *conscious and deliberate* manifestation with you simply because, throughout my life, having purchased numerous raffle tickets, I never won a prize. I was one of about 25 people taking a senior driving course in a nearby hospital conference room. When we paid for the course, we each received one raffle ticket. Three prizes were going to be raffled off after we finished the class.

This is a great time to test this Law, I thought to myself.
Does Imagination really create Reality?
Does my Imagination really have Supreme Dominion over my consciousness?
If all this is true, then I should, by this very Law, hear this instructor announce my ticket as one of the winners.

The class lasted six hours, and at the end, the instructor announced she was going to begin the drawing. My ticket number was 689. With my eyes focused on the instructor's lips, I repeatedly said to myself, "I am the winner." In my imagination, I "heard" her announce 689. Blocking out everyone and everything around me, my eyes never left her lips, as I repeated, "689, 689, 689."

I was aware that the first prize went to the woman on my left. My eyes stayed focused on the instructor's lips as I repeated, "689, 689, 689. I am the winner."

The second prize went to the woman on my right. Still, I kept my eyes on her lips, never wavering, and without even blinking, "689, 689, 689." I kept hearing her announce 689. When she finally said 689, I was still focused on her repeating 689 in my mind. It was not until she called my number for the third time that I realized I was not hearing her in my head anymore, but rather from the middle of the floor. Finally, my hand held up my winning ticket, and she handed me the prize.

20. TESTING THE LAW

At the beginning of the drawing, a gentleman sitting next to the woman on my left complained he had not received a raffle ticket. Without even looking at the prize, I handed mine to him. No prize could possibly compare to what I had just experienced—testing the Law and seeing it manifest before my very eyes. How easily and naturally it unfolded.

I was the only person in the room who knew "why" my raffle ticket won. By applying the Law consciously without doubting, my wish was fulfilled. The prize was mine. How wonderful! What a shame that I could not share my story with the others. How could they possibly believe me? I felt overjoyed! I also found it interesting that the two other winners were sitting on both sides of me. I could not explain it, but nevertheless, I wondered how that happened. There were 25 people sitting at tables arranged in a very large circle yet the two other winners were next to me. The winning numbers were not in sequence, and we each received our tickets at different times while paying for the class.

Also in the past, every time I purchased raffle tickets, I said to myself "What a waste of money. I never win at this." I could just as easily have said, "I always win buying raffle tickets!" At that time, however, I had no idea what "The Word Made Flesh" even meant.

One real creative moment, one real feeling of the wish fulfilled, is worth more than the whole natural life of re-action. In such a moment God's work is done - William Blake

I will share one last story with you regarding clothing, because in this particular arena for some reason, the manifestations appear so easily to me. This time I was looking for a pink and white candy-striped top in the usual stores I frequent. I did find one exactly as I imagined, but when I tried it on, it did not fit as well as I would have liked. This top was a large size. I would have liked to try on a medium size. However, the large turned out to be the only candy-striped top in this area.

So, I looked through all the racks, the fitting rooms, and even the petite sizes. No medium anywhere, so I went ahead and purchased the large. This happened on a Friday. When I got home, I tried the top on with every pair of pants in my closet. By Sunday, I decided that I definitely wanted a medium.

In my imagination I "saw" this very top in the same area where I found the large size. Only this time, when I checked the tag in my imagination, it had an "M" for medium on the tag.

Monday came and I put my large top and receipt into the bag and drove back to the store to exchange it for the medium that I was sure would be waiting for me. With total confidence I walked straight to the rack where I found the large top I'd purchased. There, on the same rack, was an identical candy-striped top like mine. When I turned it around, the label had an "M" for medium on it.

I took it into the fitting room and tried it on. I did not like the way this one fit either. I ended up purchasing a totally different top, but not before taking a picture of the medium top showing the "M" on the tag to remind me of this particular "testing" of the Law.

By now, I was long past trying to rationalize or explain my experiences. It happened exactly as I imagined. After testing the Law hundreds of times, I can only conclude that my imagination creates my circumstances.

That is how the Law works. You can either accept or reject your manifestation. Testing the Law daily about anything going on in my life has become a habit. I never tire of testing.

Rereading Neville's 10 books is also something I never thought I would stop doing, that is until I discovered his

20. TESTING THE LAW

lectures (which I didn't know existed) on YouTube. After listening to his lectures in his own voice, I became even more obsessed with his teachings. What a gift not only to me but to all humanity!

Several months after discovering Neville's YouTube lectures, I came across one titled, "The Wonder of it All, The Mad Mystic From 48th Street." This lecture consisted of a series of written questions and answers without audio. Question number five especially intrigued me.

The question from the audience was:

"Is it possible to imagine several things at the same time, or should I confine my imagining to one desire?"

Neville's answer, "Personally, I like to confine my imaginal act to a single thought. But that does not mean, throughout the day, that I don't imagine many things. But, instead of imagining a lot of "little" things, I would suggest that you imagine something so big, it includes all the little things. Instead of imagining wealth, health, and friends, imagine being ecstatic. What would it feel like to be ecstatic without knowing what had happened to produce your ecstasy? Reduce the feeling of ecstasy to a single sensation, <u>"Isn't it wonderful!"</u>

After reading this last part (and *hearing* it in my mind) a thrill went through my whole body. I recognized this feeling. It was the feeling I had experienced many years earlier after "firing" God. So, *this* is ecstasy? I can do this! I can do this! It's so easy. The feeling washed over me, only this time it did not frighten me. This was the feeling that had me running to doctors from 1978 to 1980 for reassurance that I was sane. I recognized the feeling. Neville called it *ecstasy*.

I taped the above part of question number five in my own voice, repeating it for half an hour, and putting it on a loop. My "trigger" to enter this state was simply to say, "Isn't it wonderful!" Every time I repeated this phrase, it sent me straight into ecstasy with goose bumps all over my body. The feeling lasted for the better part of a week. After all these years of wondering what had happened to me, I finally had a name for it. Ecstasy!

I listened to several more lectures and finally got to bed about 9:30 p.m., only to wake two hours later. As excited as I was, there was no possibility of falling asleep again. No sleeping pills would have worked. Around midnight I began listening to my taped Q&A of number five. For the next six hours, I went in and out of ecstasy listening to this tape, and repeating "Isn't It Wonderful!" at the end of the last sentence, each time the tape looped to this part.

Totally exhausted, I dragged myself out of bed and got dressed a little after 6:00 a.m. My plan for the morning was to work on my "For Sale by Owner" flyer for my condo, which I definitely decided to sell this year if I got the full price.

As I began rearranging photos of different rooms on my computer, I thought I heard a voice say, "Put the Sign Out." Dismissing it, I continued working on the photos. Tired after only two hours of sleep, again I heard a voice say, "Put the Sign Out."

"Am I imagining this?" I asked myself. "I'm really tired. I don't want to be reported for having a sign in front, even if it's small. I'll wait for the weekend and then take my chances."

I continued with the photos. After a while, needing a break, I made myself a bit of breakfast. For the third time, I heard, "Put the Sign Out."

This time, I actually answered aloud. "Nobody goes out looking for open houses at 9:00 a.m. on a drizzly Monday morning."

"Put the Sign Out," came the reply. With that, I reluctantly went outside and stuck my tiny sign in the grass next to the driveway.

20. TESTING THE LAW

"There, are you happy now?" I asked, having no idea to whom I was talking. The voice stopped.

At 10:00 a.m., exactly one hour later, the doorbell rang. A couple came to the door and wanted to see the condo. I thought I asked them if they were real estate agents. That was always my first question to anyone wanting to see the place. All I heard was "No." Therefore, I let them go through my home by themselves. I learned several days later that the husband had asked me if I was a real estate agent, and I said "No." If not for this *misunderstanding*, they would never have been allowed into my home.

This couple purchased my condo. Within an hour, the buyer came back with a contract for me to sign. Within three hours, he came back for the second time and handed me a copy of the $5,000 deposit for the full price of the condo. Escrow was opened, and they wanted to know how quickly I could move out. The condo sold in exactly one hour after spending six hours going in and out of ecstasy, listening to my tape, and repeating "Isn't it wonderful!"

Later, this gentleman told me he had not intended to drive down this particular street and couldn't quite understand why he had. I smiled at him as the thought *The Father Has Ways You Know Not Of* popped into my mind.

I remained in the state of ecstasy for approximately five days. However, it was most embarrassing at my doctor's appointment the following day. I could not yet control this feeling. Every time the doctor spoke to me, my answer was, "Isn't it wonderful!" I'm sure the poor man must have thought he had a nut on his hands. I didn't care. The fact that I finally knew what happened to me years earlier cancelled out any negative thoughts anyone could have about me.

My consult lasted for the better part of an hour. I kept trying to explain to this doctor what happened to me, but my sentences were interspersed with "Isn't it wonderful!" as I was going in and out of ecstasy on the examining table.

Then I told him about my theologian friend Jack, who'd asked me many years earlier, at the Institute for Advanced Pastoral Studies, "Maria, do you know that you are God?" When the doctor heard this, his whole body jerked.

Even in my state, I realized what a horrible mistake I'd made. This man is a fundamentalist, but I couldn't stop trying to explain. I never got to tell him my response to Jack's question. "If I'm God, Jack, then who am I praying to?"

"To the greater Whole," he replied. "We are all God, Sons of the most High. God is a plural word – Elohim, meaning one made up of others. Together, we make up the One God, whose name was, is, and always will be—I AM."

How could I possibly ask this doctor, "Dr. M, do you know that YOU are God?"

Nor did I have the presence of mind to tell him about when a friend asked William Blake, "What do you think about Jesus, who was he?" Blake answered, "Jesus IS the only God, but so am I, and so are you."

The doctor began bouncing his test vials off my body with such force that several fell on the floor. Obviously, he was quite upset. Seemingly with great effort, he refrained from commenting on my ridiculous behavior. This would be my last consult with him. To get rid of me as a patient, he did not respond to three messages I left for him with three different employees. I could not really blame him.

By the end of that week, I was able to control the feeling. Even now, I can still go into the State of Ecstasy at will by simply repeating "Isn't It Wonderful!"—not knowing what is wonderful but simply *feeling* wonderful.

These personal experiences happened over several years. However, I must confess, when I first began testing this Law, I could not keep from asking all kinds of questions.

20. TESTING THE LAW

For example, with the black dress from Nordstrom's, during that 45 minute drive home, all these questions crowded my mind. Did I create that dress because I wanted it so much? Was the dress there all along? Would this dress have existed without my imagining it in the store after seeing it on the salesgirl? Did God within me plant the thought to drive out to San Leandro to find the dress? Whom was I going to ask?

Neville, of course, who else? Once I discovered his lectures on YouTube, I kept his 10 books in the drawer. So, I went and pulled them out. There was the answer on page 166 of his book *Resurrection:*

Your Father, the I AM in you, reveals the first and last—"I am the beginning and the end," but never does He reveal the middle or secret of His ways; that is, the first is revealed as the Word, your basic desire. The last is its fulfillment—the Word made Flesh (visible). The second or middle, <u>the plan of unfoldment,</u> is never revealed to man but remains forever the Father's secret.

While this Law operates in everyone's life either consciously or unconsciously with the above experiences, I began operating the Law *consciously, deliberately, and consistently.* By now, I fully accept that I am responsible for *everything* that happens in my life. When I do not like what I am reaping and especially not remembering my sowing, I choose another state and enter it. Otherwise, my circumstances remain the same. My circumstances only "mirror" my mood and inner speech. One can enter a state either wittingly or unwittingly. That is why Blake said:

I do not consider either the Just, or the Wicked, to be in a Supreme State, but to be every one of them, states of the sleep which the soul may fall into in its deadly dreams of good and evil, when it leaves Paradise following the serpent.

Eventually, I stopped questioning. "I am the beginning and the end" became internalized and a simple and natural way of practicing the Law.

"In my Father's house there are many mansions." John 14:2
"No one comes to me unless the Father who sent me draws them." John 6:44.

Mansions are states of consciousness. States of consciousness are simply moods. I choose the mood before leaving the house. My mood determines what kind of person I will draw to me on any given day and what adventure I will experience. If I do not *consciously* choose a mood, I will return to the mood or state I occupy most often by *habit,* be it good, bad, or indifferent.

I've come a long way from the angry, vengeful God I grew up with and know God is Love from experience. Yet, after all the ongoing testing, after all the proof I've been given, at times my "old familiar friend *fear*" comes roaring back to remind me I'm still in kindergarten.

When fear does return, I consciously enter a "Kindness State" a "Forgiving State"—any state that has joy and happiness in it. Sometimes it's easy. At other times, it takes effort and determination.

And when *everything* seems to fail, I listen for the one steadfast voice that never abandons me, never betrays me, never forgets me, always puts me first, and picks me up and reassures me from within, "Fear not, I am with you always."

I close with a quote from Kahlil Gibran: *"We choose our joys and sorrows long before we experience them."*

Botsch (Batos) – Romania

Traditional clothing - Tube hat worn by single women - 1937
Mother (Mary Gramelt – 2nd from left, with three girlfriends)

**1944 Wagon Train - Exodus Out of Transylvania
Not our wagon - We had oxen pulling our wagon**

**Saxon Refugee Children – Anthering (1945-1948)
Mother's girlfriend, teacher Grete Fuhrmann & Gustav Hartig
Maria Kräutner – (standing lower right corner)**

1948 Mary & Johann Kräutner – Passport Pictures - Anthering

1946 Kräutners - Mom, Dad, Maria & Susan after Johnny was born

1947 Anthering – Part of our "gang" at the cottage
Front left – George Gramelt, Johann Kräutner
Middle – Maria Kräutner w/arm around me & holding Johnny
My sister Susan
Top – Bernard Alzner, and Dad, Johann Kräutner

www.ingramcontent.com/pod-product-compliance
Lightning Source LLC
Chambersburg PA
CBHW061657040426
42446CB00010B/1776